T0381551

O Mighty Warrior

WISDOM FOR LEADERS
AND FOR THOSE WHO MENTOR

Eric Murphy

WESTBOW
PRESS®
A DIVISION OF THOMAS NELSON
& ZONDERVAN

Scripture quotes marked (KJV) are taken from the King James Version of the Bible.
Scripture quotations marked (NIV) are taken from the Holy Bible, New International Version®, NIV®. Copyright © 1973, 1978, 1984, 2011 by Biblica, Inc.™ Used by permission of Zondervan. All rights reserved worldwide.

Scripture quotations marked (ESV) are from the ESV® Bible (The Holy Bible, English Standard Version®), copyright © 2001 by Crossway, a publishing ministry of Good News Publishers. Used by permission. All rights reserved.

Scripture quotations taken from the New American Standard Bible® (NASB),
Copyright © 1960, 1962, 1963, 1968, 1971, 1972, 1973,
1975, 1977, 1995 by The Lockman Foundation
Used by permission. www.Lockman.org

WestBow Press books may be ordered through booksellers or by contacting:

WestBow Press
A Division of Thomas Nelson & Zondervan
1663 Liberty Drive
Bloomington, IN 47403
www.westbowpress.com
1 (866) 928-1240

Because of the dynamic nature of the Internet, any web addresses or links contained in this book may have changed since publication and may no longer be valid. The views expressed in this work are solely those of the author and do not necessarily reflect the views of the publisher, and the publisher hereby disclaims any responsibility for them.

Any people depicted in stock imagery provided by Thinkstock are models, and such images are being used for illustrative purposes only.
Certain stock imagery © Thinkstock.

ISBN: 978-1-5127-8259-2 (sc)
ISBN: 978-1-5127-8258-5 (e)

Library of Congress Control Number: 2017905317

Print information available on the last page.

WestBow Press rev. date: 05/08/2017

My dear friend and mentor, Mike Calhoun, has been mightily used by God in my life. I have learned so much from him. Mike motivated me to grow in Christ, setting the pace for me. God has been gracious to bless me with the practical wisdom that He gave to Mike. I am grateful.

There are a number of young men I have encouraged over the years, and I wish I could mention each of them by name. There are two men, in particular, to whom I also dedicate this book, Iulian Avramescu and Jim Compton. I thank God for these men and pray that this book will be of great encouragement and instruction for them. May God bless the lives and ministries of all of the young men that God has given me to mentor.

Contents

Acknowledgments

What a wonderful heritage God gave to me. I thank God for my precious grandmother, Thelma Paisley, my "Mamaw." As a little boy, I listened to her prayers for me to be saved and do God's will. Her prayers brought me to Jesus Christ and still influence my life today. My "Papaw," Glen Paisley, motivated me to develop my music skills. My dear parents, Clinton and Glenna Murphy, believed in me and provided an excellent education for me. After Mamaw passed, Daddy committed to pray multiple times a day for me. My mother's encouragement and prayers, and constant belief in me, have been such a blessing.

My first wife, Lynne, played a major role in my ministry, using her many talents for God's glory for forty-two years before she passed in December 2013. God graciously gave me a new partner, Stephanie, in June 2015. Her encouragement has made this book become a reality. I truly believe I could not have written this book without her. She helped with her editing and proofing skills as well as listening to me re-live the stories in this book, giving me smiles and words of encouragement. God is so good to bless me with Stephanie's love and admiration. I am a blessed man. Thank you, Stephanie, and thank you, God.

I thank God for my four children, nine grandchildren, and for the growing number of great-grandchildren. Again, I am a blessed man.

Countless friends in Hungary who were a part of my ministry there are cherished in my memory. There are many more in Romania, Montenegro, Costa Rica, Germany, Austria, the United Kingdom, Slovakia, Croatia, Norway, Denmark, Faroe Islands, Finland, Ukraine, Italy, France, Netherlands, Portugal, Spain, Switzerland, Serbia, Poland, Russia,

Greece, Bosnia, Turkey, Israel, Kenya, Uganda, Bermuda, Canada, and the United States. Others have gone to many countries to serve, from Mali to South Korea to Australia to Mexico and to some countries that I will not mention. I thank God for all of these precious friends, praying for God's blessings upon them.

Introduction

More than once I heard a request from a young staff member or volunteer, "Eric, all of these stories that you tell us—they are great. You should write a book so we can read it again and again to learn more from you. Please help us."

Having served as a pastor, youth pastor, music minister, and missionary for more than four decades, God has taught me so much. It is time to share it with this generation as well as future generations (2 Tim. 2:2). I give God the glory for the incredible lessons that He has taught me.

O Mighty Warrior contains stories of a small-town boy who grew up to impact a country and a continent for Christ. As unlikely as Gideon, whom God called to be a leader, God will use whomever He chooses to accomplish His will. The angel who spoke to Gideon addressed him as though he had already done great things (Judg. 6:12). Gideon was threshing wheat, a simple worker doing a mundane task. But God sees us as a finished product. We do not have the ability to see the future as God does. We sputter our protests, but God sweeps them aside as He empowers us to do the unthinkable.

God searches for more who are like Gideon, with much potential but not completely developed and trained. Could it be that you are this person, this modern-day Gideon?

O Mighty Warrior is a compilation of a few of the things God taught me so that I can motivate and encourage you. Be bold, future mighty warrior!

Accountability: Good or Bad Idea?

Accountability is a good idea for those who want to grow in their faith. The ones who are hiding issues or problems think that accountability is a bad idea, resisting it with everything they have.

Opening up to a believer of the same sex can be a very healthy thing. Notice that I wrote "same sex." Man to man. Woman to woman. Otherwise, too much temptation.

There are different levels of accountability. Being accountable to a men's group or a women's group can only go so far. This kind of accountability is good, and I encourage it. Taking it to a higher level—being accountable to a staff, or having your colleagues agree to check each other about your quiet time or devotions—is excellent. Do it!

Now, let's take it to another level—much higher, much deeper. One-on-one with someone you highly respect, someone who is doing his or her best to live for the Lord—that's a special level of trust and accountability. Sounds like a mentor, right? Not always. It can be, but sometimes this is not the mentor-mentee relationship. You might choose a small group of two to four people to form an accountability group.

What I am talking about is being willing to be accountable in every area of your life—every area! Spiritual, physical, financial, emotional, and mental purity. The problem is that most men recoil from this in resistance. A woman is more apt to go to this level if she finds a godly woman for accountability. Come on, guys. Let's go. Let's take it to another level of commitment.

Some are willing to be accountable for their exercise program, using a buddy system to motivate them to stick with it. Great! Fantastic! Some open up regarding self-improvement. This is good. But they will not talk about what is going on spiritually. Some fear that if others knew they are struggling in this arena, it would be the worst thing that could ever happen. We all have our ups and downs. No one is immune to this. Your finances? Wait a minute, friend! "That's none of your business" is the usual response. However, our bank accounts or checkbooks show what we really value in life. The subject of purity—are you kidding? What man or woman does not struggle with this at one time or another in his or her life—or two times, three times, endlessly?

Okay, if you open up to one or two men or women, then there has to be an airtight agreement that what is talked about will *not* be told to others. Without this trust, we cannot be confident about sharing what is happening in our lives. There's an old joke about some people agreeing to confess their faults to each other. Everyone opened up, telling their worst sins. Finally, one person was left. Running out of the room, he yelled back to the others, "My problem is that I gossip, and I can hardly wait to tell everyone else what all of you said!"

A few of my friends have told me that they signed an agreement with everyone, promising to keep their lips zipped. One group went to a notary public to sign the agreement in front of this legal representative who signed the document and put an official seal on the paper. Those guys were really serious about trust.

With an agreement and commitment of trust in place, you can move forward. Even so, the first month or two is a bit scary, as you worry if the others will keep their promises. If so, talk about it in the group or with your accountability partner. You may find that they have a similar concern. Put your hands together, praying to God that you are making a vow. Renew your commitment. It will be a precious moment, and each of you will grow as a result.

Not everyone is ready for this kind of accountability. Work your way up to it by being accountable first to a small group. This can be staff members, a men's group, a women's group, a workout partner—any group you find yourself in. You will gain victories when you are accountable regarding your spiritual life. Ask the other members to keep you accountable and commit to do the same for them. The positive pressure of knowing you will see them again pushes you to be ready. This is good, good, good. Be as willing to admit your mistakes as to tell of your successes—with humility.

Being accountable in marriage with your partner is very important. Start with having prayer and devotions together. When your mate hears you pray, it creates security. You get to know each other better when you pray together. Listen to each other. The wife needs this so much. She is encouraged when her husband sits down to listen to her—not checking his smartphone while she is talking. The husband also needs his wife's ear and heart as he talks about what he is going through. Over the years, this will become deeper as you grow closer to each other. Make a commitment for purity.

I encourage you not to fear accountability. Make a wise choice regarding your accountability partner or group. God will guide you through this. The purpose is to become more Christ-like—our ultimate goal.

Attitudes Are behind Actions

Wise parents look for attitudes behind actions. Most parents discipline their children because of actions that are not good. It's not easy being a parent in your twenties and thirties and not having the wisdom you will have in your forties, fifties, and beyond. Again, wise parents look for the attitude behind an action. Correct the attitude, and the actions will generally take care of themselves.

Staff members do things, say things, and act immature at times. We see or hear the action or the negative words. What is the attitude behind the action? Think of it this way. Where there is smoke, there is fire. In other words, something is causing the smoke.

When we listen to a staff member say things that are not right, we tend to be upset because of these words. Slow down before exploding or losing control. What is the attitude behind those words or that action? It's like looking for the root cause. You have to look deeper than just what you see or hear. What is going on underneath?

People learn to be very creative at covering up their root problems. They will blame someone else or something else. Or they will attack, trying to intimidate. Sometimes they become defensive, or they fear you are getting too close for comfort, changing the subject to get you upset about something else and leading you on a wild goose chase.

This is a deep subject requiring more space than I'm allowed to use. Let's start with you. To help you, I'll admit that I have spent much time doing self-inspection—trying to get to the root cause of some things I have struggled with. The sooner that I get to the root cause—my rights, selfishness, and so on—the sooner I can move forward with asking forgiveness from God and forgiving myself (that's important too!). The time spent in scripture memory and reading the book of Proverbs helps me sort through verses to deal with my root problem. Would you be willing to approach it this way as well?

In other words, my belief is that if I need to correct an attitude in someone else, first I must be willing to make this change in my own life if I have not already done so. The reasons for this are manifold. Neither you nor I can lead anyone higher than what we have experienced. Are you still with me? Good! So if I can do this, you can do this. Are you willing?

Let's say a crisis pops up on your team. You are appalled at some actions or responses. Whoa! Pray to God and ask for His help as you search for Bible verses to help you find the attitude or attitudes that are behind what they are doing or saying. (After some experience, you will pick up on attitudes very quickly.) When you identify the attitude, be kind as you confront your team member.

Start with, "You know, over the years I've learned that behind our actions are attitudes. I've had to be very honest with myself, looking into my heart. No, I am not a perfect Christian—far from it. But I'm learning to be honest with myself and with God. Would you allow me to kindly ask you a couple of questions, and would you be as honest as you can be with me and with God? I kindly ask this of you." Because you have been so nice and so kind, some of the barriers have already fallen. "Could it be that what you're upset about right now is really an issue regarding _____?" (Insert pride, fear, resentment of authority, entitlement, personal rights, or whatever you think the root cause may be.)

Once you get into this, buckle your seat belt, because it can take hours before a stubborn staff member finally admits what the root problem is. Then you have to win an agreement with him or her to deal with the problem, asking forgiveness from God.

Then what do we do? Set up accountability to check up on your staff member. Continue until you see that there is growth, change, and more responsible behavior. On a corporate level in the business world, both the boss and the employee come up with a plan for follow-up. From a Christian viewpoint, we should add teaching based upon Bible principles and memory verses related to the root problem. Perhaps a combination of both would be the best.

Balancing Act: Ministry and Family or Personal Life

Who has the answer? This is a battle even for me. Sometimes I get into a project and the hours vanish as I am absorbed with completing it. Maybe your situation is similar, or it might be different.

We all have our ministry as well as our home church. You might have to supplement your income with a part-time job. Those who are raising their support while working a full-time job have a big challenge, but the situation is not impossible. If we are married, time is needed to cultivate the marriage relationship. Children, especially babies and toddlers, add a new dimension. But having teenagers in the home presents a daunting challenge.

Singles struggle with this issue, but they have different factors than those who are married. Sometimes singles get dumped on because they have more time, and the married leader overloads him or her with tons of work. All of this work needs to be completed the day before yesterday, so it seems. At the same time, single staff members really want to serve and accept the workload with a good heart. If you are dating someone, this presents a new wrinkle in handling the demands of a calendar and a daily to-do list.

Before I go any further, one thing that I have learned is that at my present age I can get more work done in a shorter amount of time than when I was twenty-five. Experience is a great teacher. So, in a certain way, I am saying that this is going to get better with time.

Getting married—the honeymoon, starting a household, both working jobs, renting an apartment, saving to build a home—it seems that the pressure increases. Building a home really squeezes the life out of both of you, but you will survive.

When the last child leaves home, the empty nest syndrome kicks in. Grandchildren—got to spend time with the grands. The aging process, with its aches and pains, throws a wrench into the works and sometimes brings everything to a screeching halt. Can you hear me saying, "Been there, done that"?

Solutions? Let's start with the most important relationship—God. The young mother can barely find five minutes to use the bathroom much less have time to read the Bible and pray. Maybe personal devotions while using the toilet is the answer. Just sayin'.

Book time in your schedule on your laptop or smartphone to have quiet time with God. In a later season of life, you can increase this time. You may be able to schedule only fifteen minutes when you have a full-time job and/or family. Just do it. Do it early, even if you have to get up fifteen minutes earlier. You are more likely to get it done early in the day than late at night when you are exhausted.

Sit down and make out a plan for your day, starting with the first things to do. How long does it take you to take a shower and get ready? Set things out the night before to speed up the process. Write down the details, including the time/preparation for breakfast and travel to work. Can you use travel time for reading, meditating, praying? Lunchtime—think about what you can do to help balance your life. One prospective missionary raised the majority of his support by using his lunchtime to make phone calls, send e-mails, and so on. He also took a quick ten-minute walk. Good for his health.

Make a plan for the afternoon, including your trip home and what you will do when you get there. Otherwise, you will waste time frustrating yourself. A married man needs to give some time to his wife—listening to her and asking about her day. Does wonders for the marriage relationship. The man is the leader, so lead. If there are children, it's Daddy time playing with the kids. The amount of time and the complexity of the activity depend upon the ages of the children.

Make the evening meal a special family time. See the chapter called "Become a Storyteller." Giving twenty minutes here and thirty minutes there in the late afternoon and early evening meets the needs of the family. Don't forget to have a family prayer time right after the evening meal or before the little ones go to bed.

It seems that the wife has twenty-some things to do before she can go to bed, while the husband is glued to the TV or is snoring away in his chair. Something is wrong with this picture. Cutting back on TV, Internet games, or trolling on Facebook will give you much more time to find balance between the ministry and the family.

Before you finish your day with some quality time with your wife, write down a plan of action for the next day. It will help you get going in the morning.

Bottom line: You have to have a plan. You are the one who sets your priorities. Put boundaries around your work so you can have a home life. When you leave work, leave it there. You're home, and you have responsibilities at home. Don't take your work with you when you get home. Focus your attention on your family. This is how you set boundaries, and your family will love you for doing this.

Balancing the Highs and Lows

Everybody has things happen to them that knock the wind out of their sails. Satan is walking about like a roaring lion, seeking those whom he can devour. Jesus promised in John 16 that we will have trouble in this world. Let's not be surprised when bad events happen, such as someone close to us letting us down.

My mother loves to tell a story of her experience visiting a shut-in. She was trying to let the bedfast woman know that she understood that her life was very difficult and that she cared. This lady quickly told her that she was so thankful for the window in her room. "Come over here and stand next to my bed, honey. Now look out my window, and you can see several homes on that hillside. I see the flowers blooming in the spring and different flowers coming up during the summer and fall. I watch the leaves come in the spring and watch them go in the fall. I see all four seasons, and I watch when it rains. You know, God is so good to give us rain. And He is faithful to have the sun shine upon us and His earth. Why, I can see so many things because of this window. I'm so thankful, so blessed."

My mother, misty eyed, told her that she had been taught a great lesson that day. She has told me this story several times, relating to me that it made a big impression upon her. The story is a blessing for me also. I thought about how this woman handled a difficult situation in her life when I went through some difficult experiences of my own. It all boils down to attitude—how we see things—how we respond to things that could upset us, stealing our joy.

Trust can carry us through tough times. Trust God, knowing that He is in control and that He has allowed tough experiences to happen in our lives—for our good (Rom. 8:28).

Recently, I went through a time of extreme physical pain, suffering from six different problems with my left ankle. The pain was excruciating. I prayed, thanking God for this suffering and pain. God impressed me to pray for people who have many more problems than what I have. So I began to pray for the believers in Syria and Iran who suffer greatly because of their faith in Christ. Families have to watch their fathers or sons beheaded in front of them as nonbelievers try to stop the growth of the church. Is their situation more difficult than mine? You better believe it is! Then I prayed for the earthquake victims in Japan and Ecuador where there was great loss of life and complete destruction in some areas. Somehow it helped me bear my pain better as I felt their pain instead.

Look beyond the present difficulty, trusting the all-wise God who is on the throne and in control. Press on! Suddenly you will feel more balanced in your thinking, and your present difficulty will be viewed in a completely different way. Otherwise, you become enslaved and overpowered by the difficulty as it gains power over you, losing your trust in God.

"Let us not be weary in well doing: for in due season we shall reap if we faint not" (Gal. 6:9).

Become a Storyteller

Throughout this book, I've told stories. Stories bring to life a point that you want to get across. People remember the point because of the story. That includes me. I relish some of the stories that my mentors and important people in my life have told me.

Become a storyteller in order to train your younger team members. It is a way of helping them understand how your ministry or business started. You know, what the early days were like. By telling a story, you can share what God has taught you (2 Tim. 2:2). Be sure to emphasize what God has done, so as to praise Him, while teaching your young colleague how to be thankful to God.

Think about some of the great stories that you have heard in the past. What was the point of each of these stories? Make a file so that you can use these stories in your messages or speeches as well as to train others. Think of keywords from these stories; it not only helps you create a title for each story but also gives you topics so that you can use the stories on other occasions. For those Twitter savvy readers, think hashtags.

I know that when I tell these old stories I am encouraged once again. Some of them I've listened to over and over. Usually, I visualize the story while it's being told. This makes me feel like I'm there watching the story unfold. I say this because when you recount a story, you will be able to tell it in a more animated, detailed way if you have visualized the story in your mind.

It's like creating word pictures. Doing so makes the speech come alive, and the audience is right with you with heightened interest. As a result, your listeners will learn more. After all, that's why you're speaking or training in the first place.

Jesus was the Master Storyteller. Reading through the Gospels, note that there is one story after another. Nehemiah must have been a good storyteller as he shared "the good hand of God" (Neh. 2:18) telling stories about the goodness of God. Can you not imagine that Luke, John, Peter, Andrew, James, and the rest of the disciples were good storytellers, telling the next generation what great things they witnessed Jesus Christ doing? After all, they were eyewitnesses. And the generation that followed told these stories to the next generation and so on.

One of the best storytellers who influenced me was Jack Wyrtzen, the founder of Word of Life. Often, I watched him tell one story after another during a message, then give an invitation, seeing incredible results of people coming forward receiving Christ. For nine wonderful years, I had the privilege of spending twenty to twenty-four days a year with Jack as we crisscrossed Florida in evangelistic meetings or concerts. Jack told countless stories to me while riding in my car, thrilling my heart. What a privilege it was for me to be trained by a master storyteller.

Go and do likewise training your team—your key leaders.

Being a Pioneer: Getting Started

When I first went to Hungary at age thirty-nine, I knew what our mission leaders wanted me to do. After all, I had seen the model organization in action when I was serving in the States—youth camps, Bible institutes, conference centers, Bible clubs in churches, sports outreach, music teams, and more.

One of the first things I had to endure was "This will not work in Hungary. It is different here. What works in the United States will not work here." Yeah, right. How did they know? Oh yes, I admit that the culture was different, and I tried to take this into account as I respected their thoughts and concerns.

My response to them was that these principles are not American. Instead, they are biblical. They worked in Brazil because they are Bible-based concepts. The philosophy of ministry was working in Argentina and all across South America as well as North America. In fact, the idea of a Bible institute, as developed by my former mission, was first organized in Brazil, not in the States. The methods were working well in the Philippines and in Australia. This was also true in Kenya, in Africa. This seemed to help them understand. I was not afraid to stand up for what I believed.

Guess what happened when I went down to Montenegro in 2006? Same thing! I kid you not. I had a good laugh over this, telling them that I had already heard these lines when I first went to Hungary fifteen, sixteen years earlier. I encouraged them to make a trip to Hungary to see what God had done in the mission there. They were not expecting this kind of response.

A similar thing happened in Romania when I went there in 1992 to get the legal paperwork done to open a mission there. A famous church leader there told me that the American methods would not work in Romania and that I should go back where I came from. He told me I would not be able to do anything there without his approval. Old Communist-style rhetoric. I looked him in the eye, telling him that he could not stop God. I did not flinch, and I meant business. There is a fine line here, but there is a time to be brave and bold. Yet totally depend upon God, being humble before Him.

In 1991 in Hungary, I had already experienced standing up to a denominational leader who had capitulated to the Communists years earlier. After the fall of Communism, there was new freedom, but the vestiges of the old system still remained. Think control, cronyism, power. The Hungarian leader demanded that I have his approval before I send any letter or newsletter to any of "his" churches in his denomination. I laughed right in his face, telling him this would never happen. Brash, cocky—not necessarily nice spiritual attributes but just what needed to be done at that time. I am a different man today, as I have aged and grown in the Lord.

Confidence. The Hungarians told me again and again that I was confident. Perhaps the difficulty of living during the "Difficult Years," as they called the years under the control of the Russians, had destroyed their confidence. I cannot imagine what that pressure must have been. I have listened to stories of both Hungarians and Romanians who had to endure that system, that stress. It was not easy, to say the least. Please do not misunderstand me. I am not criticizing these dear people. In fact, I found many brilliant Christians in these countries—impressive people.

You have to have confidence. Be careful; do not be arrogant. Confident about what? About the vision that God has given you to do in your country. Confident that your philosophy of ministry is based upon God's Word and that it is based upon a solid model that you have seen in action.

Visualization. When I stood inside the building that would become our meeting room, I visualized Hungarian young people laughing at the crazy skits, singing their hearts out, listening to my messages, raising their hands to mean that they had prayed the prayer to receive Christ, and coming forward to meet with their counselors. I walked into the dining room, and I could see in my mind the teenagers walking in as I would be singing a song. I saw them remaining standing as I prayed, thanking God for our food. I heard the buzz of conversation around the tables during the meals. I saw the platters full of food with plenty to eat. I walked to the area where I planned to build basketball courts, and I could see young athletes competing. As I walked over to the lake, I made a plan to create a beach, and I saw, in my mind, kids splashing water and having a fun time. On the soccer field, I saw that we needed to level the field and build new goals. I knew Hungarians loved their soccer. Walking through the woods, I thought about young people getting alone with God in prayer. What a joy to see all of this come to pass! To God be the glory!

Work ethic—all of this could not have happened without God's help and a work ethic. God loves work. He gives us work to do. You have to put in lots of hours of work to realize, to bring about what God has called you to do.

Loneliness. When you are the pioneer, the first one on the field before you have a team or before the other team members arrive, there will be bouts of loneliness. Take it to God in prayer. Keep the vision that you have before you all the time and keep pressing to get it done (Phil. 3:13–14). Take time to read the Word, to pray in order to feed yourself. The outer man is perishing, but the inner man is renewed day by day (2 Cor. 4:16). Keep on keeping on. You will reach your goal with God's help.

Don't give in and don't give up. As I have written in this chapter, don't give in to the naysayers, the doubters, or to the ones who tell you that you will not be able to do what you have set out to do. I may be a little red-faced as I admit this. When I was in my twenties and early thirties, I used to tell negative people, "Eat my dust." Doesn't sound very spiritual, does it? But on the inside, I knew what God had called me to do, and I was determined to do it no matter what.

Sometimes the negative, whiny people are part of the group that is closest to you. It is a test. God is testing you to see if you will do what He has given you to do.

Looking back on what God did in Hungary, Romania, and Montenegro, there was one test after another, as God tested my heart and the evil one, Satan, tried to stop and derail me. Just look at what God did! Not Eric Murphy. God! To God be the glory!

Be Willing to Use Yourself as an Example

Jesus is our example—His sinless life, His obedience to the cross, how He spoke kindly to people, His parables and teaching—truly He is our supreme example. The apostle Paul acknowledged this in his preaching and writings. Yet Paul knew the importance of being an example to those who traveled with him on his missionary journeys as well as to those to whom he ministered and served. Paul was bold enough to write in Philippians 4:9, "Those things, which ye have both learned, and received, and heard, and seen in me, do: and the God of peace shall be with you."

Well, of course, Paul could write such a bold statement. After all, he was *the* apostle Paul. Now which one of us, you or me, wants to step up to utter the same statement, "Those things, which ye have both learned, and received, and heard, and see in me, do." Uh, are you hesitating a little bit? Big gulp. Me too. Am I worthy to say this? No. Are you? I'll let you answer that question.

Yet God wants us to be examples for others. Have you ever said, "Oh my, many of the great heroes of the faith have died. Who will take their place?" Well, I have thought about this. Could it be you or me? Are we the ones to step up to be examples to those within our spheres of influence? Feeling queasy in your stomach? No, none of us feel worthy. Having talked with some of the great heroes of the faith before they died, I felt more at ease when they told me that they did not feel worthy but that they realized God wanted to use them as examples to others who were following them. Bold! Cutting-edge boldness.

With fear and trepidation, I realized that I needed to live Philippians 4:9 as a leader. I want you to do the same. Let's do it with humility. There are many younger in the faith who need us to do this. The old heroes are passing. Let's teach the next generation and the one coming up after them.

One way to do this in our preaching and teaching is to be willing to admit our failures and what we have learned from them. Perhaps you have noticed that some leaders try to give the impression that they are perfect. Nothing could be further from the truth. Instead, I have noticed that when I admit some of my struggles and what I learned from those experiences, it connects with young people as well as adults. In doing so, an example is set.

This teaches believers to deal with their faults or problems rather than gloss over them. In doing so, I am saying that the things that you have learned, and received, and heard, and seen in me, do these things. Then you will have the peace of God in your hearts. See my point? I have to be willing to change when God confronts me with a Bible verse or passage, a sermon, the gentle admonition of my wife, a close friend's admonition, or from a good Christian book that I am reading. Take it to God and change by repenting and asking for His help. Then I need to be willing to share this with other believers through a changed lifestyle as well as in my preaching, teaching, or counsel that I give. Or here in this book.

The boldness is in being willing to confess, change, and manifest the new behavior. It's not the idea of standing at the pulpit loudly boasting that I am the example. The boldness is in living the example, so I can preach and teach this at the pulpit. Sharing what I have learned, being willing to admit failure and telling how God helped me is the message that people need today. So, we live out Philippians 4:9 so those who are watching, listening, and following can do what the great apostle was trying to convey.

Be bold, new hero of the faith!

Catch Someone in the Act of Doing Something Good

Then tell him or her about it!

How's that for a different spin on working with a staff? Usually leaders operate with a negative mentality of trying to catch people doing the wrong thing and correcting them. Of course, there is a time and place for this. But I encourage you to try this one on for size—catch a staff member in the act of doing something good and tell him or her about it.

After the initial shock wears off, the team member will have a broad smile on his or her face, thinking, *Wow! Now this is really different. My leader noticed! He really noticed my performance. Yes!*

Why? Glad you asked! People absolutely love praise. They love it, love it, love it. Give genuine praise for a good performance, a good deed, a positive action. Phrase it something like this:

"Josh, man, you did something today that I really appreciate. It was great."

"Excuse me?" Josh asks, mystified.

"You had the PA system and all of the equipment set up at least one hour early. Everything was in place and ready to go at the right time. Excuse me, even before the right time. I really appreciate this! Good job!"

"Sure, uh, no problem," stammers Josh as he beams at you.

"And what's more, you roll up the cords just right and tape the wires to the floor to make certain that no one trips over them. You're the man! I love it and appreciate your good work. Thank you."

"You bet! I love what I do. Hey, thanks for telling me this."

Can you see Josh standing taller already? He is pumped and feels appreciated. Now, you got it, and I think you understand. So go catch somebody doing something good. Dish out the well-deserved praise, and your staff will operate at a higher performance level than ever before.

Okay, I know you may have one team member that you struggle to find something good to praise him for. I am not surprised by your thoughts. Every staff or team has members who are at various levels of maturity and development.

So you pray, asking God to help you find something positive, something good. Think about a new shirt, shoes, something he is wearing and tell him it looks good on him, that it looks sharp. Or just the fact that he took a shower, washed his hair, and looks refreshed. If this fails, notice how he walks, smiles, handles himself. Maybe it was his comment in a staff meeting that helped others in the meeting. Tell him how much you appreciate this.

"Great comment at the staff meeting. I really liked what you said."

"Boy, you look sharp today. Amazing what some hot water and soap does for all of us. You're looking good."

"Love your new jeans … sharp, really sharp."

"Hey, thanks for holding the door for the senior citizen. Great move. I saw her smiling at you."

I'm serious. Catch people doing the right things and tell them about it. Don't gush but tell them because this teaches them what you want them to do. When they know you are watching and that you are appreciative, their performance will improve.

Far better to praise than to criticize. (See the chapter called "How to Confront a Staff Member.")

Change the World through Prayer

Do you believe that you can change the world through your prayers? I do. Which world? Do I mean the big world, planet Earth? Yes. Your world as well. The world you live in and those who are around you. Family, neighbors, colleagues, or classmates. This is what I call your sphere of influence. You can change your personal world through prayer. And you can effect change all around the world.

God put something in my heart a few years ago. Pray for the nations. Specifically, pray for the closed nations, that is, closed to the Gospel. Pray for spiritual breakthrough into these strongholds of Satan. Then pray for the rest of the nations around the world, for those who minister to students, church planters, music (concerts), sports, and for the believers who live in these nations. Outreach to students can bring about change in an entire nation. It's happened before, and there are books that tell these stories. Why not now? Today? Church planters have reached small towns, large cities, counties, even an entire nation just by starting one church. This church started other churches. Why not pray for these dear people who are church planters? Sports and music are two of the best ways to reach young people. Some are using the Internet to reach people in many nations with creative programming, articles, and podcasts. Why not pray for much success with this type of outreach? Christian radio is another example. Youth camps—so many young people make decisions at youth camps in a neutral environment outside of the church itself. Some people move to foreign nations to work alongside nationals in order to build relationships. It is important to pray for all of these endeavors for God's blessing. The promise of Isaiah 55:11 is, "So shall my word be that goeth forth out of my mouth: it shall not return unto me void, but it shall accomplish that which I please, and it shall prosper in the thing whereto I sent it."

Praying for certain nations where there is persecution of the believers is so important to me. My heart aches for the believers in Syria, Iran, and Iraq to name a few. Parents are made to watch their children beheaded in front of them. Or for children to watch their parents' heads cut off by a fanatical Muslim filled with hatred. I pray for these precious people. God is at work even though this is hard for me to understand. I agonize over their suffering. Yet the church grows despite this persecution.

If you saw some of the names of famous people that I am praying for, you would wag your head in disbelief. "No way, Eric. You are praying for the impossible." Well, God put this on my heart. Talk about sphere of influence—I will never be able to reach the friends of these famous people. But if they become believers, one by one, *they* can. God is at work using me to pray for rich, isolated people who hide behind protective walls to keep people like you and me away from them. God can penetrate these walls, and I'm praying that He will do so. I find it interesting that the Creator of the universe wants to use people like you and me to accomplish His work, His plan. Mind-boggling.

Can you imagine the early church members, who had been being scourged and persecuted by Saul, when they heard that he had become a believer? They recoiled in fear, in disbelief. More like, "I'll believe it when I see it. Until then, I'm keeping my distance." Saul was like a mad man, hell-bent on exterminating all of Christianity. God changed that! Could it be that some of the early believers prayed for Saul's salvation? Hm-m-m! Probably this happened. At least a few of them prayed for his conversion. Think I should keep praying for my list of the rich and famous? By the way, I'm praying for their souls, not for their money. God will deal with that after He brings them to Himself.

There is a list of people who need salvation, spiritual change, or growth—another list of some who are very sick and a list of heartbroken parents whose older children have strayed from God. It's fun to pray for a number of young men who have great potential. Then there are friends who need to make important decisions, and I pray for wisdom for them. Praying for our extended family members—for the LIFE ministries in various nations—for pastors name by name—for those who are in leadership transition—for our supporters—board members and advisors—my goals and projects—those that I mentor—and more. What an honor it is to pray for these people and for needs.

Success? I praise our great God that there are several "Prayer answered!" notes next to some of my prayer requests. This encourages me so much to keep praying. There are many requests where nothing like this has happened, but I continue to pray.

Sometimes I feel like I'm digging a ditch in hard ground filled with rocks. It's hard work. I hope you will allow me to say that sometimes it feels like dull, boring work. But you keep on because you know that the job is not finished. Keep digging the ditch. When

I read in somebody's book that he feels this way at times, I raised my hands in the air. "Thank you, Lord, for letting me know this. I'm not alone." What I'm saying is that this is hard work. Not every prayer time is like this. Every now and then, there is a reward—prayer answered!

Praying for the nations by continent or geographic area, I pray for South America, Central America, Asia, Australia and nearby nations, North America. Recently, I was praying for Europe, nation by nation. When I came to Bosnia, I had a terrible satanic attack taking my mind to something that made me angry. It was like my mind was a battle zone filled with landmines and one of them exploded. Putting my hands over my face, I repented as I wondered aloud how I could even think of something so awful. Suddenly, it hit me—Bosnia is a stronghold of Satan. There are some good people serving there, and they are stirring up Satan's wrath. That got my mind back to praying for this nation. It happened again when I was praying for the Scandinavian countries. Again with Germany, of all places. I know precious people in these countries who are believers. Do you recall in the book of Daniel when the archangel Michael was delayed because of a great spiritual battle with the prince of Persia (modern-day Iran)? There is spiritual warfare in high places. It is my conviction that we need to pray for the nations.

Something is happening because of all of this. God is changing me. Spending time with Him in prayer changes you. It's great, wonderful. There are lots of quotes from some great books written on the topic of prayer. I liked one in particular. "Prayer. Just do it!" We can read books on prayer (I'm not saying not to do this), but the main thing is just to do it, to pray.

Now do you believe that you can change the world through prayer?

Chasing Skirts: Your Ticket to Disaster

Working with young people is a wonderful ministry. They have so much energy—abounding with potential. How fulfilling to see spiritual growth in their lives as you watch them grow up year after year.

You know, I've noticed that there is a fine line between the spiritual and the physical. After a campfire meeting, a very special spiritual experience, the teenagers usually hug each other. Sometimes the hug is lingering. Uh-oh! The line has just been crossed from the spiritual over to the physical. Her young bosom pushed against a teen boy's chest. A male doesn't need only his fingers to feel things—his chest suddenly becomes very, very sensitive to touch as he realizes what is touching his chest. Oh no, we have a problem here.

Never, never, *never ever* do this with one of your pretty young teenage girls or any girl for that matter. It is so innocent, at first, even a bit naive. Naive on her part and stupid on yours. Listen, men, you can get your mother's little idiot into trouble so fast, quickly tempting you.

Let's back up just a little bit. If you have been noticing that the pimple-faced thirteen-year-old girl has begun to "fill out" at fifteen or sixteen, let me ask you, "Just what have you been looking at?" The Old Testament teaches us to make a pact, a commitment with our eyes to not regard evil. (Job 31:1 says, "I made a covenant with my eyes not to look lustfully at a young woman" (NIV).)

Young girls will be blessed by your ministry, your character, your drive, your positive spirit—your good looks. They want to be married someday, and some of them wish they could marry a man just like you because they admire you so much. Some ten- to thirteen-year-olds have a crush on you, fantasizing what it might be like to be married to you. If this kind of thing builds up your ego, get a life. Come on, you're in danger if you show that you like this attention with your eyes lingering on certain parts of their anatomy. Well, you just bought your one-way ticket to disaster. Don't do something stupid, ruining your marriage and your ministry. Too many good men have done this.

What do I do? What do I do?

Paul told us men to "flee youthful lusts" (2 Tim. 2:22). Know what "flee" means? Literally run from it. Don't come near it. Avoid it. Hear me and hear me well, it's not worth it. You are playing with fire, which will destroy you. Your teen girls deserve much better from you.

Here's what to do: When you look at a member of the opposite sex, look her in the eye. Give a young lady or any woman respect by making eye contact with their eyes, not with her bosom, not her bottom (taking a lingering, lustful look when they walk away), not trying to see how far you can see up her skirt or checking her cleavage when she bends over. Good grief. Honor her with your eyes looking into her eyes with a pleasant, wholesome smile on your face. Keep your eyes there, making eye contact. She will appreciate this so much.

Think of making yourself become a safe zone. Committing your eyes to God daily, asking for His help, you protect the young ladies in your ministry by choosing purity at all costs.

They are now safe. In fact, do this with every woman. If you are married, ravish your wife with your love. She's the limit, the beginning and the end. That's it. No other female. Not even an emotional affair that you hide in your private thoughts. If you are single, still make this commitment. God will reveal the one that He has for you. Commit yourself to purity so that you will be pure for her.

Then, get out there and minister to your girls and your guys with a totally different perspective as unto God. Not like a certain man I met when I was thirty-five. Same age as me, handsome as he could be, smart as they come, talented, gorgeous wife, beautiful children, seminary graduate from one of the finest seminaries in the world, great speaker, witty, athletic—you name it, he had it. He blew it all because he chased skirts. He lost it all because he refused to pursue purity. Shattered life, ruining the lives of those closest to him—so, so sad.

Your choice.

Choose Someone to Mentor

In 2 Timothy 2:2, it says it all: "And the things that thou hast heard of me among many witnesses, the same commit thou to faithful men, who shall be able to teach others also."

Someone invested in your life and helped you to get you where you are. Now do it for someone else. We all know about Paul's relationship with Timothy, along with others. So who is your Timothy?

I've found that it is good to have someone in your life who is about ten years older to serve as one of your mentors. Pick out someone who is at least ten years younger than you and pour yourself into his or her life. Or fifteen to twenty years younger. That is what this book is all about, and this is why I spent hours and hours writing this, just for you and for those you will mentor.

Buzz through the chapter called "Looking for Potential." You can mentor someone your own age or slightly older than you. Thinking of building for the future, be sure to choose someone younger than you so you can teach him or her the ropes, sharing the wisdom that God gave you. This is vital for the development of the body of Christ, as we need younger men and women to carry on the Great Commission (Mt. 28:19–20).

Maybe it goes without saying that men should mentor men and teenage boys, whereas women are to mentor women and teenage girls. Just in case. There, I said it. Take heed.

Make a mental list, or if you're like me, write down two or three names of potential mentees. You're the mentor, and the one you're training is your mentee. Commit this list to the Lord in prayer. Not just once—take a week to pray daily, more than once a day. This is super important. The Lord will give you peace about which one to approach first

(Prov. 16:1–3, 9). It's a war zone out there, a battlefield, and we need God's help to equip young soldiers.

The approach:

"Hey, Jeremy, how's it going? Man, you're looking great. How do you do it?"

"Oh, hi. Hey, thanks. How are you?" Jeremy replies.

"Super. God is good. Life is good. I'm happy. Thankful! Jeremy, do you have time to get together for a Coke?"

"Yeah, I guess so. What's up?" Jeremy is seeking more information.

"Nothing special. Just wanted to connect with you. See how you're doing," you say as you spread your arms out to show you're not hiding anything, making him feel at ease.

"Yeah, sure. When?" Jeremy relaxes.

After you set a time and place, think about your opening lines when you get together (and keep praying). Make general chitchat for a couple of minutes, such as asking about how school is going or how his job is going. You want him to feel at ease. Then tell him that you have noticed him and that you are impressed with his potential. He'll probably roll his eyes or sputter. Smile as you look him in the eye. "Jeremy, I'm serious. God has put you on my heart, on my mind, and I've been praying for you. Earlier in my life, an older man invested some time in me, and I've always been thankful for this. To be honest, I feel that God is impressing me to do the same for you if you're willing."

Set a definite day and time that works for both of you. Let him know that there will be some fun times, such as going to a game or an arcade. I'm a big fan of walk and talk because taking a walk together, you are side by side, moving as you're walking and talking. It's less of a threat than sitting directly across from each other, which somewhat looks like a confrontation.

If a teenager is involved, it might be a good idea to give the parent a call if you know the parent or a short, personal visit if you've never met. Let the parent know what your intentions are to set his or her mind at ease. My experience is that most parents appreciate a big brother or big sister to encourage their son or daughter. Give your phone number in case they have any questions or concerns.

Now what do you do? Check out the chapter called "How to Mentor."

Dealing with Discouragement

It happens to every leader. The demon of discouragement can make or break you. Some people, due to their temperament, languish in it. Others deal with discouragement from time to time. So how do you pick yourself up?

King David was subject to bouts of discouragement. One time his men talked of stoning him after the enemy attacked their stronghold at Ziklag, taking away all of their possessions, wives, and children. Only days earlier, when David made a remark that the water was sweet to the taste in an enemy-occupied town, some of his finest men risked their lives by sneaking into enemy territory to bring back this water. Now, they wanted to take his life. Oh, the ups and downs of leadership.

David had reason to be upset as well because the enemy had taken his own wife and family. In 1 Samuel 26:6, it gives us the secret—David found strength in the Lord. Next, he prayed to God in verse 8, asking what he should do. God told him to go after the Amalekites and that he would succeed. It took nearly two days of battle, but David and his men were victorious, taking back their wives, children, and possessions.

The first thing to do is to think about the goodness of God. Things may be difficult right now, but review your life, thinking about the times God helped you when there were bad times earlier. Think about the lessons you learned. Search the Word for promises that God is with you, even holding you by your right hand.

One thing I've learned to do is to thank God. A thankful heart puts me where I need to be in relationship with God. The book of James tells us to be joyful when there are tribulations or trying experiences. Try that one on for size. By the way, it will "fit." I promise you. Already, your spirits are beginning to lift you up from despair and hopelessness.

Pour your heart out to God. David gives this example to us time after time in Psalms as he agonized before God, telling of his problem, asking God for help. Each time he did this, David finished the chapter praising God. God will listen, and He will care. God knows you because He made you. He knows how you are wired. He simply wants you to come to Him with your problems, asking for His help. When you do this, thanking Him, you will find that He lifts you up and empowers you to continue.

Note that David did not have anyone to turn to at that moment. His men, even his top men, were so grieved that they wanted to take David's life. David was in dire circumstances. He had already cultivated the habit of going to God with his problems.

What did God do when Elijah was so discouraged that he wanted to die? God fed him, made him lie down to sleep, fed him some more, and gave the man three more jobs to do. Did God reject him? No! A resounding no! He will not reject you or me when we get down. We serve an incredible, kind, and loving God.

What do you want to call this? The Ziklag method? David encouraged himself in the Lord, and He prayed to God, asking for direction. It really doesn't need a name or title. Just do it. Want to wallow in self-pity and discouragement? No, it stinks. It makes you feel bad about yourself. This only prolongs the negative feelings. The sooner that you do what David did, the sooner you will become encouraged and motivated.

People can be so fickle. They can turn on you so quickly. But somebody has to be the leader, and you are *that* person. If David had not turned to God, encouraging himself, what would have happened? As a result of David's response, they were able to get back everything that they had, plus the spoils of the Philistines, one of David's enemies. The Amalekites had raided the Philistines, plundering their countryside. They got back what they had lost, plus even more.

God blesses the man who comes to Him with his problems, asking for guidance. As a result, he is encouraged rather than discouraged. This encourages me. You too?

Death of a Key Leader

Dan Bubar died as a result of a trailer becoming disconnected from a truck, coming across the median, and striking his vehicle. He had no idea what hit him.

I received a phone call about midnight telling me that Dan was in life-threatening condition in a hospital in Budapest, Hungary. After driving one hour, I arrived at the hospital, meeting the father of one of our Hungarian staff members, my assistant, Ildiko Barbarics. After meeting with Ildiko and the neurosurgeon, I learned that Dan had a minimal chance of survival, noting that the surgeon held his forefinger right against his thumb—zero chance of success. But he promised to do his best in the surgery.

After comforting those who were present, I went outside for some fresh air and to pray. It was May 1, 1996. The standards in hospital care in this former Communist country were not as high as they are today. Noticing an open window, there was Dan lying on a bed with his head wound showing. His head was grotesquely swollen. I could see his crushed skull and see brain matter. I think God allowed me to see this to let me know just how critical his condition was.

Have you ever prayed and felt like you could not even take a breath? Finally, I cried ever so softly, begging God for my young friend's life.

What does a leader do in this situation? After prayer, my next decision was to call his parents. Dan was single, twenty-nine. His father, who happened to be my boss, was in Canada at the time. His mother was in a midweek church service, so I called to the church, asking the person who answered to get me the pastor. He came at once to the phone, being called away from the pulpit area, as he had not yet started his message to the congregation. I asked him to get Dan's mother to the phone and for him to remain to comfort her. Agreeing, he sent someone to bring her to the office. My stomach was in knots as I tried to prepare myself for this difficult moment. Of course, she wanted to know all the details, and I answered her truthfully, mentioning that the surgeon thought there would be next to no chance for survival. That was one of the most difficult phone calls I have ever experienced in my life.

After the phone call, I prayed some more before returning to the emergency room lobby to wait for a report from the surgeon. The doctor was grim, telling us that he did his best. Dan was hooked up to a respirator as we waited to see if his body would respond to the surgery.

No private room. No ICU. He was in a room with nine young men who had recently suffered traumatic brain or spinal injuries. One young man was lying on top of twelve pillows lined up, turned perpendicular to give him more support. Each one had a horror story connected to his injuries. Our Dan was near the door, hooked up to life support.

What to do? "Oh, God, help me!!" My voice filled with love, I began to softly sing songs and quote Bible verses to him. Praying that he could hear me, I hoped this would help him. If nothing else, it helped me. Dan's father called later, asking for details, telling me that they could come in three days, as it was difficult to get things organized to travel. And you lose a day in travel from the States to Europe. He asked if I could hold the fort. Yes, of course. I did not want to be anywhere else. They came as fast as humanly possible.

Driving back to our ministry center, I prayed aloud for mercy, for healing. After showering and getting fresh clothes, I met with the staff to share what had happened. They were stunned beyond measure. They cancelled classes at our Bible institute so the students could meet with the staff for a long prayer meeting. Everyone dearly loved this incredible young man.

Continuing the vigil of staying close to Dan's bed, I asked God for a miracle. This request was denied by the Holy One who knows what is best for our lives. There are many other details—his parents arrived—they organized Dan to be airlifted to Germany where there was excellent medical care. Finally, the German doctors concluded that the brainwaves were being created by the breathing machine, that he was actually brain-dead. They said the Hungarian surgeon had done a good job and they could not have done any better. The decision was made to discontinue the medication. He was officially with the Lord in a matter of hours.

It was devastating, absolutely devastating. I had poured several hundred hours into this young man, mentoring him. Maybe it was more than a thousand hours … God knows. In the back of my mind, I wondered if I was helping train the man who one day would become my boss, the international director of our mission. He had *that* kind of potential. It was a privilege.

What did I do? I was alone, as my wife was in the States for medical care. I told her to remain there because there would be a memorial service in Upstate New York where Dan's home church and the mission headquarters were located in Schroon Lake. This would be after the memorial service that we had for Dan in Hungary. Yes, I met with staff, and we prayed. During the quiet moments in the daytime, I played the piano and sang songs to restore my soul. I wept more than I ever had in my life. I could only imagine what his dear parents were going through. At other times, I was on my knees by the couch in my office, praying. I could not keep from softly groaning as I prayed. I was broken, deeply broken. I loved this young man dearly.

Deciding to trust God, I pressed into Him. I reviewed my life, noting how God had worked in the past. My only conclusion is that God is good. Whatever He does in our lives *is* for our good (Romans 8:28). Though I could not understand why this had happened, I trusted God that He had a perfect reason. Based upon these principles, I could take the next step into the unknown. The loss of Dan created a huge void of leadership in our mission. Now, looking back on this more than twenty years later, I can tell you that God was with me through the days and years that followed. God raised up others to stand in Dan's place. Teenagers came to Christ because of Dan's death and his testimony. Many dedicated their lives to God to serve Him like Dan had faithfully served.

You may or may not go through the difficult experience of losing a key leader. If you do, press into God. Trust Him. Get past the fact that you may never understand *why*. Keep serving. Keep moving forward one step at a time. You will learn so, so much if you do this.

P.S. Please read my chapter on "Death of a Spouse."

Death of a Spouse

"But it was so that the works of God might be displayed in him" (John 9:3 NASB).

My wife, Lynne, suffered from multiple sclerosis for twenty years before going to be with the Lord on 12/5/13. She suffered from pain almost the entire twenty years, gradually becoming worse and worse. She was in terrible pain the last four years of her life, having almost unbearable pain in the final two years. It was difficult for her to bear this pain, and it was difficult for me to watch her suffer.

Many times I prayed, asking God to take away the pain or to make it more bearable. Never once did He answer these prayers in the affirmative. At no time did the pain abate or cease. What He did do was give us grace to bear the suffering. As a result, God changed me, breaking me, making me a better man. I am the man I am today largely because of this process. I thank God for what I could not understand during those days. Now I understand much better. Slowly I began to realize that this happened so that the works of God might be displayed in Lynne's life.

Praying Away versus Praying Through

In Marc Batterson's superb book, *Draw the Circle*, he writes, "We are so fixated on getting out of painful, difficult, challenging situations that we fail to grow through them. We fail to learn the lessons God is trying to teach us or cultivate the character God is trying to grow in us. We want God to change our circumstances that we never allow God to change us! So instead of ten or twenty years of experience, we have one year of experience repeated ten or twenty times."(1)

Marc Batterson tells us that we need discernment when to pray "get me out" prayers or when we need to pray "get me through" prayers. I went through this during Lynne's suffering, realizing that God was at work in my life. Choosing to press into Him, I asked God what He wanted to change in me. One day, He answered quickly. "Tell Lynne that you love her more than ever before." I was stunned. Surely, there has to be more, something else. Pride, it's bound to be my pride plus something else. I waited. Silence. Then the thought came to me again, stronger this time. "Tell her that you love her more than ever before." With that, I got my cell phone out to call the caregivers at Lynne's assisted living facility. Lynne could no longer hold her phone, needing someone to hold the phone to her ear so she could receive my phone calls. I was in Dallas, Texas, on ministry business, but I knew this message could not wait a second longer. God had spoken to me.

This change brought me closer to God because I told Him I love Him more than ever before. Lynne's suffering brought me closer to God.

Mark Batterson writes, "Can our prayers change our circumstances? Absolutely! But when our circumstances don't change, it's often an indication that God is trying to change us."(2) I agree 100 percent because of my own life experience. Thank you, Lord!

Sometimes God delivers us from our problems; sometimes God delivers us through our problems.

Fortunately, this story has a sweet ending. Be sure to read my chapter, "God Has Restored What the Locusts Have Eaten."

Developing a Teachable Spirit

When I think of a teachable spirit, the words "gentle" and "meek" come to mind. Open mind and an open heart as well. Arrogance, manipulation, pride, closed-mindedness, harshness … these words are just the opposite.

You can learn to be teachable by using your daily devotions, prayer, and Bible reading with the attitude of asking the Lord to speak to you. Tell the Lord that you will respond immediately, as soon as possible, to change what you are doing or how you are acting. As God ministers to you through this, immediately thank Him for speaking to you, convicting you to change. Then do it, change it. Now.

Open yourself to allow those in authority over you to help you grow in Christ. Doing so helps you develop a teachable spirit. Obey your authority and seek to do everything you are asked to do. And do so with a sweet spirit.

Take notes during sermons in church services. This disciplines the mind and heart to be open to instruction and correction. Review the notes after the meeting to see what you need to change or do in your life. You are slowly developing a teachable spirit.

If you argue with authority, your boss, or supervisor, you do not show that you have a teachable spirit. An argumentative spirit is the antithesis of a teachable spirit. Your spiritual growth will be stunted. Do you love to debate? Enjoy arguments? Always have a conflict going on with someone else? Look deep inside of yourself before you answer these questions. Do you always have to win? Have the last word? If yes to any of these questions, you do not have a teachable spirit. Rather, you are willful, arrogant, and conceited. You are closed-minded and hard-hearted. May I kindly ask you to repent? Ask God to search your heart and try your ways, as David did when he prayed to God. If you are the leader, those under your leadership will suffer because they will learn your ways.

On the other hand, if you have a teachable spirit, you will inspire your staff to develop this precious quality. This is what you want. This leads us to an important principle. Nothing will change until you *want* it to change. You will not grow in Christ until you *want* to do so. This principle is true for getting in shape, toning the body, weight loss, achieving any of your goals, improving your life or that of your loved ones. You have to *want* it badly enough that you will make sacrifices, change your lifestyle, or discipline yourself. When you really, really *want* something, your mind will find ways to get what you *want*. You see, your will has to be broken, disciplined, or controlled. That's when the mind takes over, to overcome your will. For us as believers, we have the power of the Holy Spirit helping us in this process. But the Holy Spirit does not move until you allow Him to work, that is, until you *want* change.

Bottom line, you have to *want* to have a teachable spirit. Nothing changes until you change your *"want to."*

At the time of this writing, I have been using a certain devotional book with the mind-set that as soon as I realize the Lord is speaking to me about whatever He wants to change in my life, I immediately change, repent, enact, or do. I had to *want* to do this. As a result, God is really speaking to me about numerous things, causing new spiritual growth in my life. I am more teachable because of this. Praise be to God!

Do you *want* this?

Don't Count Your Chickens before They Hatch

Before we could open our youth camp in Hungary, we had to do extensive renovations. Put in a sewage system—install bathrooms and renovate the dorms—drain the lakes, dredge them to clear all of the buildup over the years and reinforce the banks around the lakes—build a basketball court—dig trenches and build a concrete canal to install new water and heating pipes. It seemed like an impossible challenge.

A donor from Texas pledged a gift of $75,000 to help with this project. A foundation in the state of Maine promised $50,000 to install the sewage system. On the basis of these promises and being under pressure to meet the deadline of opening our first week of summer camp in June 1990, we signed the contracts to start the massive construction and renovation.

We received the donation from Maine, but the other donor changed his mind. Stunned, I made a phone call kindly asking him to reconsider, explaining that we had already signed the contracts. He explained that his wife wanted to contribute to another project in another country. He closed the conversation by saying, "Sorry."

In present-day dollars, the value of this donation would be three to four times $75,000. It was a major blow. As I thought about it, an old saying, "Don't count your chickens before they hatch," came to my mind. I prayed, "Oh, God, keep my spirit sweet. Don't let me become upset or bitter. Help me with this crisis." God helped me with my spirit, but no money came in to meet this need. This made for a larger crisis in that our mission leaders struggled to handle the payment schedule. Our headquarters made funds available to pay the contractors' bills when they were due, but I had to pay back the main mission organization, signing an agreement to this effect. Small amounts were paid almost every month after this, yet it took a long time just to pay $10,000 back, much less $75,000. Eventually, we were able to pay it all back. Praise the Lord!

After going through this experience in my ministry as well as a period of time in my twenties when I was in debt, I've often said, "I hate debt." Never have I gone back into debt after I got out of debt at age twenty-eight. Never did our mission go into debt again after the experience in 1990. Never ever! If God did not provide the funding or if the donations slowed down because of an economic crunch in the States, we simply shut the project down, waiting and praying until God moved. By the way, I had a celebration in my office when the big debt was finally paid off. I thrust my right arm into the air shouting, "Hallelujah, the debt is paid. Thank you, Lord!" I finished it up with a war whoop.

Doesn't the Bible teach us to count the cost before we build? Yes, Luke 14:28. Well, we did this. But we did not have the money in hand, in the bank, not all of it. With the stress of calendar days passing, we needed to get the construction started to have a chance of opening the youth camp on time. What happened with this donor changing his mind has influenced me to not start a project until the money has been given and we have it in the bank. Ouch! Tough lesson but a good one.

God tested my heart again in 2015. The potential donor in Texas was still on our mailing list, and I had written to him each year since 1990, asking him to kindly consider whatever project we had going on at the time. I received a note from his secretary in 2015 asking me to take the donor's name off both of my e-mail and mailing lists. Complying, I responded with a kind note to tell him that he would not hear from me again. I prayed for God to keep my spirit sweet. He did.

Yes, God met the need—in His time. Make a plan, count the cost, make the appeal to your donors, and wait for the money to be donated. Despite all of that pain and difficulty, I am thankful to God that we opened the youth camp on time, which was a miracle considering all of the work that had to be done. I praise God that 168 Hungarian youth came to Christ during the summer of 1990. That's 168 good reasons to be thankful rather than angry or bitter.

Don't Quit

Losers quit. Winners keep going.

Everybody has ups and downs, great times and tough times. If you're down, you're not alone, because many leaders have waded through difficult experiences that took the wind out of their sails.

No, I'm not immune to this either. However, I rarely was discouraged until my first wife started her physical decline, battling MS for twenty years and three months. The last three or four years of her life were horrible as she endured nonstop pain. Again and again she told me that she wanted to give up, feeling as though she couldn't bear this anymore. The reality is that there was nothing she could do about her physical situation. She slowly lost the use of her fingers first, then her feet and wrists. Next, her legs. Then, her arms. Complete, total loss. She lay in bed motionless, except that she could turn her head back and forth. Finally, she lost her ability to speak. Poor thing, her body had already given up, so she was talking about her spirit, her determination and drive.

Me? Oh goodness, well, I *had* to keep going on because she needed me. Placing her in an assisted living for the last thirty months of her life, as I could no longer take care of her by myself (hurt my back and left elbow very badly lifting her), I visited her as often as I could. Standing in the hallway outside her door, I would stand as tall as I could, putting a smile on my face. Then I entered her door with my booming voice. "Hi! So good to see you! I missed you!" Same thing almost every time—she was laying there sobbing. Sure enough, she started the "I give up" statements as she despaired for her life. I could *not* give up. (See my chapter on "Death of a Spouse.")

There were a couple of times earlier in my ministry that I allowed another person to discourage me until I realized this was my fault. I told myself to choose not to quit, not to give up. Then I counted my blessings. My spirits began to rise. No one can make me quit or give up. I chose to press on. "Brethren, I count not myself as apprehended: but this one thing I do, forgetting those things which are behind, and reaching forth to those things which are before, I press toward the mark for the prize of the high calling of God in Christ Jesus" (Philippians 3:13–14). These verses helped me so, so much. So did Galatians 6:9, "And let us not be weary in well doing: for in due season we shall reap, if we faint not." Actually, I began to thrive because of adversity, because I pressed into God, and He blessed me. Jesus promised that there will be adversity in John 16:33. Slowly, I began not to be surprised by difficult experiences, because the Lord told us it would happen.

Then, in my late fifties, my wife's disease worsened. Previous bouts with adversity paled in comparison with this. I had to go deep inside of myself to review my marriage vows, deciding not to give up but to press forward. Pressing into God as never before, I found that He gave me strength to continue. I'm totally powerless without God, so I give Him the praise.

So, what did I do when Lynne passed on December 5, 2013? I knew it was coming, and I prayed, thinking about what I would do the day after her passing and the week after this and the month after this, and so on. Making a commitment to God and trusting Him for the future, I did not give up. To God be the glory!

I've described ministry situations and the death of a spouse. That's enough to make any man have thoughts of giving up. Take it to God! Press into Him as never before—on your knees or with your hands up in the air with your palms up, praying, "Oh, God, I need you so, so much. Help me, God. Show me what to do. Give me the strength to keep going. I sense that you are not finished with me yet, so please show me what is next." He did! And He will do it for you too!

Elijah was ready to throw in the towel after the spiritual battle on Mt. Carmel. It had been one of the best days in the history of God's people as they finally responded, shouting together, "The Lord, He is the God! The Lord, He is the God!" They routed the prophets of the false god, Baal. But Elijah stumbled when the wicked Queen Jezebel told him that he would suffer the same fate as her false prophets—death—if he was not out of town by sundown. Running into the wilderness, he was totally distraught and despaired of his life. When God confronted Elijah, he told God that he was the only one left who had not bowed his knee to Baal. God responded that there were 7,000 others who had not bowed to the false God. He whined to God that he wanted to die, but God did not kill him. Instead, the Almighty fed him and caused him to go to sleep. After more rest and food, God gave Elijah three major jobs to do. Instead of letting Elijah quit or die, God gave him more work to do. Amazing! God so understands us when we are down and disheartened. He does *not* give up on us! So, should we give up on God?

By the way, things are usually 7,000 times better than what we think they are. That's what God said! We let things get out of focus, and we have a pity party. Get your focus back on God. Get some rest and get back into the game. Elijah did!

"If thou faint in the day of adversity, thy strength is small. For a just man falleth seven times, and riseth up again" (Prov. 24:10, 16).

(Psst! See my chapter called "God Has Restored What the Locusts Have Eaten.")

Do the Next Thing

Elisabeth Elliot Gren was a personal friend, along with her husband, Lars. She is now with the Lord. For a number of years, Elisabeth was our featured speaker at the ladies' conferences we organized in Hungary. Usually, the meeting room was completely full with quite a number standing up in the back along the walls—standing room only. It was a great pleasure to have them in my home again and again.

There are a number of things this veteran missionary taught me. She had suffered greatly, losing her young husband as one of the five missionaries who were murdered by the Auca Indians in Ecuador in the 1950s, captivating national attention in the USA. She returned with her young daughter to reach the very Indians who had taken the life of her husband. Most of them accepted Christ as a result.

One of the most outstanding lessons was the title of one of her talks, "Do the Next Thing." Elisabeth was a no-nonsense person, dedicated to her task as a speaker and author as well as a mentor to younger women. I recall her looking deep into my eyes when I commented about doing the next thing. "You will grow as a leader if you learn to do the next thing no matter how difficult it may be. Simply put, *do the next thing*." Her gaze did not waver. She had a faint smile on her lips, yet she was as serious as could be. With a smile on my face, I held eye contact for what seemed to be half of eternity. Finally, she ended her penetrating look into my eyes with a nod of her head and a nice smile as she looked down at her coffee and brought the cup to her mouth for the next sip. She was dead serious, and I firmly believe that she lived according to her precepts.

I have thought about this memorable moment a number of times over the years—each time I looked at my to-do list, marking the next item with an asterisk, as I set about to get it done with full resolve to finish the task.

What is the next thing that you must do? Get it done and you will feel a surge of victory within your soul. You will find that you get more done each day, drawing a line through each item on your personal to-do list. Immediately, you will determine the next thing to do. Do it and you will achieve much for the Lord.

Aren't you thankful that Jesus Christ did the next thing when He faced the cross?

Do Well in Little Things

Young people aspire to become great leaders, to do great things. One thing I have noticed is that some young adults seem not to like doing what they deem as unimportant, trivial assignments. They want to get involved with the big jobs and do so right now. I'm not talking only about present-day millennials. I saw this before anyone had thought about the name millennials. I watched this with boomers and Gen Xers. This is probably true of every generation.

Luke 16:10 talks about how being faithful in little things leads to being faithful in big things. There is no other way to learn this. Proverbs 22:29 says that a person who is diligent in his work will stand before kings—that is, he or she will be promoted. Bosses love people who are diligent, taking care of small tasks. When they see this, they hand out bigger, more important projects. There is no shortcut, no bypass. More importantly, God loves diligent workers. Our Father is watching, and He sees those who excel in small things. You will be trusted to handle big things at a later time if you are faithful in little things now.

Go the extra mile. Do the next thing. Do it now! Excel in little things, doing it for God. When you receive a task, don't worry about how little or how big the job is. Do it for the glory of God. In doing so, you honor your leader, and you honor God. God will take care of what happens next.

Enthusiasm Is Contagious

Some people are naturally enthusiastic because this is part of their personality. For those who are more laidback, introverts that I call Phlegmatics and Melancholies, there are things that you can do to increase your enthusiasm. Years ago I read a couple of books written by master salesman Frank Bettger. He had to push himself to be enthusiastic in his work. He gives the following tips:

—Sit in the front row. Where will you normally find me sitting? In the front row. The only time I sit in the back is if I am in a foreign country and I need translation to understand the speaker. There are no disturbances in the front row. This may sound a bit harsh, but losers sit in the back row.

—Walk 25 percent faster. This really works. Picking up your step gets more moving than just your body. You are more alert and more motivated. The mind is signaling to the body that it should be in action mode.

—Speak up! Question/answer time—be ready with some interesting questions. You are seen as a leader by others. You are more alert when you concentrate on listening to the speaker. Take notes.

—Look people in the eye. This is important in meeting people for the first time. Give eye contact as they talk. Use their name when you speak to them to help you remember names as well as give value to the other person. In meetings, make eye contact with the speaker. Keep a warm smile on your face. As a result, you push yourself to be more enthusiastic.

—Give a firm handshake whether you are a man or a woman. You are not trying to squash their hands, showing your great strength. But a firm handshake signals to the other person (along with looking at them in the eye) that you have inner strength and confidence. This confidence boosts your enthusiasm.

—Smile big! It takes fewer muscles to smile than it does to frown. A warm smile is a winner. Helps to keep you positive. Works for me!

Although Bettger did not mention this, I would like to add one to the list. Sit up! Don't slouch in your seat during a meeting or when you are meeting someone in an office. Do these seven things and you will motivate yourself to be more enthusiastic.

Taking a look at the inner person, having a right relationship with the Lord helps one to be enthusiastic. What else? Be thankful. This does wonders for the spirit, for the heart. This is the spiritual secret to keeping a positive attitude and being enthusiastic in your life for the Lord. One more, give praise to God. This goes hand-in-hand with being thankful. God loves praise. Praise is a win-win, a blessing for you and a worshipful experience with God, which pleases Him.

First Priority: Your Wife

Crazy in love—that's probably how your romance started with the one who became your wife. I can't say this strong enough: keep it that way!

Romance your wife even if you've been married for twenty, thirty, forty years or more. Never stop romancing her! Tell her how much you love her, and do it often—more than once a day. Shower her with words of appreciation and gratitude. Leave special love notes around the house or in her lingerie drawer. Your wife will flip out over these notes. They mean so much to her. Not just the notes but also your words. Did I mention hugs? A romantic wink? A lingering caress? A warm smile? A piece of chocolate or some ice cream? Mail her a romantic card. Sweet text messages with romantic emoticons. Did you ever think about taking a shower and putting on cologne? Shave, dude! Clean up your act, and she will notice.

If you have young children, find a time that will be your special time to be intimate with your wife—late, early, middle of the afternoon during the kids' naptime. By the way, Romeo, go slow at first. I know, you get your jets revved and you want to be satisfied. Everything happens quickly for you. Not sure if you realize this or not, but women are different from men. A woman is aroused slowly with snuggling, caressing, lots of kissing, tenderness. Don't be selfish all the time—uh—how do I say this? Let her enjoy herself first. Oh my, we say things more openly in these modern days than when I was a young man. Okay, now that I've said it, carefully heed my words.

When you satisfy your wife's sexual needs, she will really, really take care of you. If you "go first," night after night, she will start to lose her interest, and your satisfaction won't be the same as it was when you were first married. Your line about asking her if she wants a back rub will lose its effect. Make this mutually satisfying, and you both will be happy.

Wait, wait, wait—we're not done yet. Listen, Mr. Go-Go-Go, pray with your wife. Not just at meals. Have a set time that you pray with your wife. I know this is difficult with small children or even big kids in their teens. You need to have Bible reading and prayer with your wife and children, *and* you need to find even just a few minutes to pray alone with your wife. This is so tough to do when you have little babies. Just hold her in your arms and pray for two minutes. Three minutes is a luxury because by this time one of the babies is crying his or her eyes out.

What do you do if you haven't been praying with your wife and you've been married for four or five years? Do like I did (ouch, this hurts—self-confession). Put your hands on her shoulders, asking her to forgive you for not praying with her. (She is probably very frustrated with you already, so she may be quite dubious about your sincerity.) While you are holding her shoulders, tell her that you feel so awkward and that this is a struggle for you because you're embarrassed. Then, take a stab at praying with her. When I did this in my mid twenties, I felt like a failure. I asked God to forgive me and asked my wife to forgive me. I did it, and it was easier to pray with her the next day, the following day, and so forth. Why is it that men, even men in the ministry, struggle to pray with their wives? Duh!

Here's what I learned. There is a close connection between the spiritual and the physical (sex). When you meet your wife's spiritual needs, you will be blessed with your physical needs. I promise you, this is the truth. If you shut her out spiritually, she will not respect you. You need respect so much. Okay, it may be time for you to put on your big-boy pants. Time to grow up, fess up, and really love your wife. She has sacrificed so much for you, bearing and raising your children. Not to mention doing the laundry, preparing meals, looking after countless details. And you think if you earn the money (we call it "bring home the bacon") that you're done with your responsibilities? Give me a break. Get yourself by the shoulders and shake yourself as hard as you can. Stop it! You're being selfish. Love, love, love this special woman that God gave you.

You know what you need to do? Same thing that I do. Yeah, me! I praise God often, saying, "Thank you, Lord, for my dear wife! You have blessed me abundantly! I am so happy! I love her so much and she loves me so much! Thank you for giving us to each other! You are at the core of our relationship, and we both love you, adore you, and worship you. Thank you for Stephanie! You are so, so good to me, to both of us."

This is exactly what I do, and I do it often. What's my point? Proper attitude to God and to my wife, along with proper self-talk. Then, I lavish praise on Stephanie. She is so grateful. She is really with me in this mission, and she is happy to serve with me. Want the same in your marriage? Go for it!

"Husbands, love your wives, even as Christ also loved the church, and gave himself for it" (Eph. 5:25).

From A to B and from B to C, Etc.

Colossians 1:28 says, "Whom we preach, warning every man, and teaching every man in all wisdom; that we may present every man perfect in Christ Jesus."

Breaking down discipleship into bite-size portions, I think of it as getting a person from point A to point B. Then from point B to point C and so forth. Usually most of us want our disciples to really "get it" and to do so quickly. Sorry, it takes a lot of time to grow young believers. So, let's look for incremental growth steps, small steps of improvement.

Have you ever taken time to think and pray about what your young disciple needs to learn next? After he or she learns this, what should he or she learn next? Have you written this down? This will help you to think it through and make a plan. Maybe you have a general idea in your mind, but having a written plan gives us a guideline to work from so we can disciple effectively.

The idea of presenting every person perfect in Christ Jesus is a daunting challenge. Perhaps we can have the goal of getting a person to the point where he or she can disciple someone else. When you get them to this stage so that they can disciple others, you will have accomplished what Paul had in mind in 2 Timothy 2:2, "And the things that thou hast heard of me among many witnesses, the same commit thou to faithful men, who shall be able to teach others also."

Then you can disciple disciplers, those who disciple others. Now you're really cooking! You're on fire! What do the disciplers need from you? How do you get a discipler to the next level? Back to the A to B and from B to C idea. Maybe you are motivating him or her to get from R to S or S to T. Do you have a plan for this?

We cannot move anyone higher than where we are. We have to continue to grow, to feed ourselves. There is no substitute for this. Dig into the Book. Have a prayer journal with a growing prayer list that features lots of praises, "Prayer answered!" Continue to memorize scripture verses. Do you have a list of people you are working on to bring to Christ? Are you reading a Christian book right now? Do you have the next three planned out to read? Which book of the Bible are you reading right now? Are you reading through God's Word on a regular basis? Have you ever read the Bible through in one year? Have you done this twice in one year? Do you read a chapter of Proverbs each day? There are many questions to ask yourself. So, are you pushing yourself to stay ahead of the ones who are under your care?

This is a never-ending task. Presenting every person perfect in Christ Jesus is the long-range goal. It will happen as we are ushered into eternity. Meanwhile, let's chase the goal—every day—today and tomorrow.

Get More Information before Responding

You cannot believe your ears when you hear what someone in your ministry has done or said—that is not right. Quickly you respond, only to find that you did not know all of the facts. If you only had known—you would not have blown up or responded so hastily or harshly.

Proverbs 18:13 teaches us to get more information before responding. "He that answereth a matter before he heareth it, it is folly and shame unto him." Having learned the hard way, I now understand it is wise to slow down and pray. Then ask for more information before responding. You will save yourself much trouble and avoid causing heartache and hurt in other people's lives.

After I pray, I ask myself what other factors might be involved. I try to look at the situation from another viewpoint. As I slow down to think it through, I return to the Lord to pray again, asking Him to give me wisdom to know how to respond or how to ask the right questions that will bring out the facts.

A word to the wise: get more information before responding.

Giving Your Vision to Others

Years ago my boss said something that stopped me in my tracks. "No one on your staff will have the heart for the mission like you have, but train your leaders to come as close as possible to this."

Blink, blink. I sat there in silence, soaking in his words. I thought of two of my men, how committed they were. I thought of four more who were almost as close in their commitment. I was perplexed at first. "Boss, I have two men who are passionate about our mission. Their work ethic is out of this world."

He responded, "Yes, I know them well, but listen to me," repeating what he had told me. "So focus on getting them as committed as you possibly can."

Why did he tell me this? Does he see something that I was not seeing? Thinking on this for a few days, I began to realize that he was right. Perhaps he was teaching me how to prepare leaders for future roles. Maybe to prepare one of them to take over the leadership role in the mission. Then I thought about one of these two men who did not respond when a sudden windstorm was followed by drenching rain. Our mission was situated in an old castle in Hungary. Two or three times we had severe wind, bringing reddish sand from the Sahara Desert in Africa all the way to Hungary. Everything was covered with this red sand. Cleanup was a big mess. One of these men walked past me as I was rushing to close the windows in the castle. He kept on walking to his office, oblivious to the sudden crisis. Duh!

To his credit, this man came to me later, slapping his hand against his head. "Eric, I don't know where my brain was. I should have helped you close the windows. I am so sorry."

Putting my hand on his shoulder, I said, "My young friend, be ready next time. I may not be here at that time."

Do you become frustrated with staff members who don't pitch in to help? Why do they walk right by without lending a hand? One day I heard a guy on my team commenting that somebody should do something about a problem that he noticed. Coming up behind him, I said, "And you are that someone. When you see something that really needs to be done, do it even if it is not in your job description." Startled, he hurried quickly to take care of the situation. I gave him a big smile of approval. I think he learned an important lesson.

But my boss told me that I would not be able to get key leaders to have the burden, the passion, the vision for the mission like I have. That bothered me. To this day, his words are still true. Some made it to 95 percent, 98 percent, 99.75 percent. No, I'm not being critical or unappreciative of their efforts. Maybe my comments bother you right now. Hopefully, you can get others to the 100 percent level. If so, great!

What do we do to teach our staff to excel in their job descriptions? What about teaching them to take care of things not covered in their job description? Working with young leaders in their twenties, we need to keep in mind they are immature at times. Okay, you may have been more mature when you were twenty-four, but I'm certain that you will admit that you had to learn a lot of things in your twenties. And in your thirties. Quite frankly, I'm still learning in my sixties.

First, do you pursue excellence? In your relationship with your wife or husband? With your children? With your job? Do you work as if you are reporting directly to Jesus Christ? That thought will push you in the pursuit of excellence. You have to learn this before you can teach this to others. Don't be frustrated with your younger team members if you're not setting the pace.

Do you get together with your staff weekly? Do you meet with your top leaders one-to-one? What are you teaching them? Tell them what you want. Compliment them when you see that they are doing what you want. Communicate! Praise often! When you confront a staff member, do you do it in private or do you peel his skin off in front of his colleagues? Hard to motivate someone who has been rebuked in public. It's just not right.

Realize that this process will take a long time. After all, Christ will not give up on you or me, as Paul promised in Philippians 1:6.

Personally, I teach that there are four temperaments—personality traits. The writings of Tim LaHaye and Florence Littauer teach these temperaments. A Choleric Leader is a great motivator but can be so caustic, so harsh in his rebuke. Cross him one time—you are never forgiven. A Sanguine Leader is a great motivator, but he wants to have fun and overlooks actions that really need attention. A Melancholy Leader can motivate, but he is a perfectionist. If someone does not match up to his expectation, he rejects the person with vitriolic criticism. Then he is sullen and depressed the rest of the day. The Phlegmatic Leader can motivate others and is loyal to the end. But he hates confrontation and runs from it.

None of us are just one temperament. Rather, we are a blend of two or three, with one of the temperaments being somewhat higher than the other(s). A commitment to become more Christ-like, for us leaders, will result in us becoming more Godly leaders. And we can teach this to our team members over a period of time. It is a never-ending process. Don't lose heart. Keep working on the goal of encouraging every staff member to grow in Christ (Col. 1:9–10, 28).

God Has Restored What the Locusts Have Eaten

Nestled in the short, prophetic book of Joel is a lesson on locusts. God uses locusts as a means of punishment and judgment. When an army of locusts comes to an area, there will be total destruction of every plant and tree and all grass. I'm told that the buzzing sound of a horde of locusts' wings is an incredibly loud noise.

God promised in Joel 2:25, "And I will restore to you the years that the locust hath eaten, the cankerworm, and the caterpillar, and the palmerworm, my great army which I sent among you."

Earlier, I shared that my first wife died because of complications due to MS, multiple sclerosis, on December 5, 2013. Nineteen months later, God restored what the locusts had eaten. Joel 2:25 uses the future tense with the word "will" referring to a prophetic event. I am personalizing this verse for my life. What I'm sharing with you is that God, my Provider, did restore what the locusts and other insects ate. What do I mean?

On June 7, 2015, I married Stephanie. Oh my, we are so happy and very much in love. Yes, God has restored what the locusts have eaten. He did it for me, and He did it for Stephanie. Her dear husband, Jerry, was a very good man and very good to her. Stephanie checked him into the hospital thinking that he would get better soon, but he did not. Four months later, Jerry went to be with the Lord, dying from COPD, a disease of the lungs, in March 2014. She suffered great loss and went through a very hard time in her life. God brought us together, beginning our friendship in early 2015. After much prayer, we both felt led by the Lord to join together in matrimony.

Stephanie was saved when she was ten years old, living in southern Indiana. During her teen years, she wanted to become a missionary, but life took a different turn for her.

Little did she know that she would marry a missionary later in life. Just to make certain, when I proposed to her, I did so while we were both on our knees having finished prayer together. My proposal included two questions: "Stephanie, will you marry me, *and* will you serve God with me?" I had told her earlier I didn't want to be like a traveling salesman going away on trips to the mission field, returning home to tell her what had happened. I wanted her to be with me in this mission, doing it together with me. Her response? Yes and yes! Praise the Lord!

You will experience loss in your ministry, in your life. Loss of property, land, car, staff members, possessions—you name it. Don't despair—the Lord will give it back at a later time. And it might be better than what you lost. (You just have to read my chapter on "The Lord Giveth and the Lord Taketh Away.")

Let's think of great loss as being a test for you. "And the Lord said unto Satan, Hast thou considered my servant Job, that there is none like him in the earth, a perfect and an upright man, one that feareth God, and escheweth evil?" You probably know the story of Job. Satan put the whammy on him, taking away everything he had, including his children. The devil did spare Job's wife so he could use her to harass Job, and she performed that task very well. (Sorry, ladies. Your roles in our lives are so, so important. Your Godly input is very valuable to us, and we are thankful for you. Job's wife did not do this for him.)

We all know the end of the story, that Job was faithful to God, learning to fear and respect God more than ever before. We are happy when we read that God gave everything back to him twice over—that is, double. Wow! What a happy ending.

Do you remember what happened right before God gave back what Job had lost? It's very important. This might have been the biggest test of them all for Job. God told Job to pray for his three friends, that God would forgive them for their sins. God said that He would only hear Job's prayer on their behalf. They had criticized Job over and over. Criticism is hard to weather, to bear. Especially from your closest friends. They didn't know what was going on behind the scenes regarding Satan being given permission to cause great loss in Job's life, hoping he would curse God and die. However, they certainly jumped all over Job to attack him and criticize him, judging him. You probably can come up with names of some people you know who would fit this description. All of us have probably had this happen to us.

If God asked you to have a proper attitude toward your accusers and pray for them, would you do it? No, I can't prove this, but I'm convinced that if Job had refused to pray for them, resenting what they had done to him, he would not have been given everything back. Do you suppose that because Job did offer a sacrifice for these three friends, praying for them, that this was the reason that what was returned was doubled? Scripture is silent on that, but I may be on to something with this line of reasoning. God searches deep into my heart just like He does yours. He knows our innermost thoughts, and He wants our hearts to be totally focused on Him, compliant with His will. When God sees this, He blesses abundantly.

Hope you remember this when you suffer great loss. Hope you pass the test with flying colors.

Hey, did I tell you how happy Stephanie and I are? God is good!

God Is at Work

Trust—can't live without it. God is searching our hearts to find trust. Do we have it when one of our children stumbles or a grandchild hates God? What do you do when faced with an insurmountable problem? Whine? Complain? Be angry? Sulk? Rebel against God? Blame God? All of the above?

We are all human. We have our ups and downs. When we turn to God with trust, we begin to embrace the difficulty rather than complain about it. God is pleased when we trust Him enough to say, "God is at work."

"God is at work" means this: God is at work.

I can't explain why "bad" things happen to "good" people. Or why "good" things happen to "bad" people. One of the Bible authors tells us that God gives rain to the good and to the evil. I trust God that He is good and what He does in our lives is for our good, according to Romans 8:28. Who can explain why devastating things happen in our lives at times? The natural person asks, "Why?" The wise, spiritual person quietly states with confidence that God is at work. We can't fathom these things, but we can trust God to work behind the scenes to accomplish what He pleases.

What about the rebellious staff member who left in a huff? Speak kindly about him, privately praying for him to yield to God, trusting that God will work in this person's life. What about your son or daughter who is against everything you stand for? Cuts you to the bone. Trust God that He is at work to bring about change, even though it may take years to accomplish this.

Speaking of change, I've noticed God is at work on Eric Murphy when there is adversity in my life. Not only is He working on me, the Creator is at work in the lives of individuals who are part of the adversity. This includes those who are watching my life. The same is true for you. Trust, trust, trust!

God will take care of the future. He will bring about the change He desires. We may never know exactly what happens, and we don't *have* to know. We simply trust that God is at work.

Do you have someone or something in your life that you need to trust God for? Trust Him as never before. The result? An inner peace that keeps you moving forward. Yes, God is at work.

Growth Is Not an Option

Googling "Growth is not an option," I found that this phrase is used in various industries, personal growth and leadership. I'm not sure who first penned these words, but research shows that no matter if you are a businessperson, entrepreneur, economist, author, counselor, or a Christian—growth is not an option. Neither you nor I are exceptions to this rule.

Looking back over my life, I see growth patterns at different ages and stages. I struggled to get going, find my place, in my early twenties. However, my thirties were characterized by tremendous spiritual growth. My life changed drastically at age thirty-nine when I moved to Eastern Europe, to Hungary, which was about to explode with change with the Berlin Wall coming down. So, my forties found me with workdays of fourteen to fifteen hours, day after day, building and developing a major mission center. My spiritual growth continued, but all of the hours necessary to pour into peoples' lives, renovation and construction, fundraising, meeting national leaders, preaching—well, it seemed that I drew upon the foundation I had laid in my thirties. Yes, I fed myself spiritually during my forties, but it was not with the intensity that I pursued God during my thirties. During my thirties, I spent one or two hours a day in my walk with God. In my forties, it was a struggle to squeeze in thirty minutes. The year before I moved to Hungary, I read fifty-two books. My first year in Hungary, I was so busy that I struggled to read fifty-two pages. The schedule was horrendous. Then again, I was the one who made the schedule.

During my early fifties, I continued this unbelievable schedule, living on five hours of sleep, and then God moved me into a different work. I had more time to seek God, but the big challenge was the drastic change in my wife's health during my fifties. Ministering to her needs, I became sleep deprived and exhausted. I pressed into God, trying to understand why all of this was happening. This continued into my early sixties until God took her to heaven at age sixty-three. I pressed into God as never before, which required a major investment of my time to do so. From this summary, I have learned something very important.

Develop correct spiritual habits and learn to do a deep evaluation of my spiritual life every year or so. In my twenties, my mentor taught me to feed myself spiritually by having a daily quiet time of Bible reading and prayer. I followed his example of memorizing scripture. Oh, this has helped me so much over the course of my life. Daily reading of Proverbs has been a wellspring to draw from again and again. I can tell you that what I learned from scripture memory and Proverbs got me through my forties and early fifties when the demands upon me were unbelievable. It was like a deep reservoir for me to draw from when my time was so limited. I am not saying that it was right that I allowed my time for God to be limited. It was a unique situation, and God helped me. I thank God for a mentor who got me started on correct spiritual habits that have carried me through life. I continue these habits until today with no plans to stop in the future. Either you grow and move forward, or you pause and lose ground.

Deep evaluation of my spiritual life: what I mean by this is that I would pray, asking God to speak to me as to why my spiritual life had become stale or why I was not growing like I had before. Writing down my thoughts, I was brutally honest with myself, noting what I wanted to change. You absolutely have to have these times of self-evaluation. Then you start afresh, asking God to help you with the changes that you want to make. A quote from an old evangelist of yesteryear, Fred Brown, has always stuck with me: "The Christian life is a life of many new beginnings." Pray using 1 John 1:9 and begin anew with vigor.

Do you know what happened each time I did this? A tremendous spiritual growth spurt! Sometimes you feel like you hit a plateau in your spiritual growth or you hit a wall. Bam! My mentor used to talk about this as he taught me to do a spiritual evaluation so I could start climbing again in my pursuit of God. When the next plateau or staleness comes, simply do it again. How many times have I done this over the course of my life with Christ? The laptops I've used over the years must contain fifty or more files of my new plans for spiritual growth. I have old notepads with handwritten notes, chocked full of my renewed attempts to get my act together. To tell you the truth, I just did this again a few days ago—one more time. I'm sure I'll do this again before the year is over. Do it as often as you need and don't become discouraged. Ups and downs are part of spiritual growth.

What do you change? Focus on a new area of spiritual growth, such as scripture memory. Or read through the Bible in one year. Try writing out your prayers. Or get alone and pray aloud. Change your posture in prayer, getting on your knees or on the floor. Get out a songbook and sing songs as part of your personal worship. Look up verses that are the inspiration behind songs. Look to heaven and pray with your eyes open, smiling to God. Pray as you walk, whispering your prayers. Meditate as you read a psalm, taking time to listen to God. Choose a certain chair or room to have your quiet time and prayer. In warm weather, get outdoors for your quiet time. Write in a notebook an entire chapter from your Bible, writing it out word for word in your handwriting. Choose a new Christian book, marking every five pages with a pencil mark, and set a goal to read five pages a day. At the end of the book, do your personal book review, writing down what you have learned. Take sermon notes when your pastor is preaching. Read them over when you get back home to do a review. Write a list of five character qualities that you need to improve. Concentrate on one each week for five weeks, choosing a themed verse or two for each character trait. At the end of five weeks, repeat one or two. If you still need to improve, choose some new ones and do this for another five weeks. Or seven weeks, eight or ten. Read a chapter from Proverbs every day for a month. Continue this for a year. Mark meaningful verses in your Bible and commit some of them to memory. I haven't even scraped the surface yet. Be creative, asking God to show you what to focus on.

From time to time, I have used a chart that one of my mentors used. It's called a spiritual growth chart. Make a spreadsheet listing various areas of spiritual growth in the left column and thirty-one columns across the page to check off your progress on a daily basis. I use this when I really want to get serious, challenging myself to be accountable with a visual—something that I keep on my desk. I do not like to leave blank spots that I have not checked as being completed. It is a great motivation for me. Another way to be accountable is to share your goals with an accountability partner who will ask you tough questions when you get together. That is a great motivator as well—iron sharpening iron.

Hate to Make Phone Calls

Once I get started, I love 'em!

Now, isn't this the silliest thing? I hate to make phone calls. Dread them. Put them off. Absolutely ridiculous.

Then, when I finally make the first call, I become energized and race to the second call on the list. I dive into the third one. By the fourth call, I'm on a roll. It seems that talking with people to get them to do this or that gets me pumped up.

I'm being painfully honest. It's the truth. Oh, that first call. Oh my. How difficult it seems to punch in the numbers to get started.

One thing that has helped me is to use a chart or spreadsheet to stay on course to get the job done. I think this is because I love to see my progress on paper. It helps me to recruit when it's time to recruit people to help with a project or ministry. It helps me with fundraising. Or to book meetings or whatever I'm working on.

Another tip is to list my phone calls at the top of my daily to-do list. If I tackle the most difficult thing to do for the day, it helps me get more done the rest of the day. So, I use the thing that I seem to dislike the most to get me motivated to get the rest of my list done for the day.

One of my former bosses told me that when I called him, I was always business first, and then I would be friendly. It was his way of teaching me the importance of friendly chitchat at the beginning of the phone call to show interest in the other person. Good advice that was well taken. Maybe the phone call to him was the first one on my list because I was making myself get started with my phone calls. I don't remember exactly, but his advice was just what I needed. It's a matter of building relationships, which is so, so important.

Sigh. Excuse me, I have to make a few phone calls. Gotta go. Sigh.

P.S. Just a short footnote—I wanted to get back with you to tell you that I just finished with my third phone call, and I'm in orbit. Gotta run because I can't wait to talk to some more people!

How to Choose a Mentor

With the idea in mind that often more is caught than what is taught, who are you watching? Who do you admire? What is it that you admire? Write down your thoughts, then pray and ask God for wisdom and examples to consider. Can you come up with a list of five people who you would like to use for role models in your life?

Keep in mind that you will notice negative traits or deeds here and there. No one is perfect, and this includes you as well. But there are some great examples to consider today. As you have noticed, there are both positive and negative examples in the Bible. Who is your favorite Bible character? Or your top ten in the Bible? Write this down, listing beside their names what sticks out to you. Pick one of them, asking yourself if you know someone today who reminds you of this favorite character in the Bible. If your list is growing, then you are on the right track.

Do you personally know one or two on your list? Great. Watch them from a distance for some period of time. Don't be disappointed when you see some cracks in their armor. We are all human, and all of us who are seeking God come to Him again and again, asking Him to forgive us and change us. But you will find some qualities that are godly, and you want these qualities in your life because you want to grow. Maybe God will give you an opportunity to speak with someone on your list. Brave enough to ask this person to mentor you? Go for it! Even if he or she reluctantly has to decline because of a busy schedule, you can still watch from a distance and learn much. If the person agrees to mentor you, then you have a great blessing ahead of you.

You may never be able to meet some people on your list. She may be a speaker on a TV program, or he may be a great pastor in another country. You can use the Internet to follow them, checking their websites and blogs or reading their books and articles. There is nothing wrong with distance learning. Can you imagine the thrill of the New Testament believers in the early church when they received a letter from the great apostle Paul? They looked up to him because they owed their salvation to him because he came to their city earlier. Or they had heard wonderful stories about him from other believers. They listened to the reading of the letter in the church service, straining their ears to capture every word. They waited for their turn to read the letter with their own eyes after the meeting. He was their hero, their spiritual leader, and they learned so much from his writings, advice, and instruction. We now know his writings as part of the New Testament, inspired by God and blessing our lives in this modern day and time.

Keep a log of what you are learning from your mentor. Write a list of questions to ask. Choose wisely which questions to ask.

Now that you are on your way to building a relationship with a mentor—who are you mentoring or discipling (2 Tim. 2:2)?

How to Confront a Staff Member

Think about a sandwich—two pieces of bread, with meat or cheese and the trimmings in between.

To build a sandwich, you need a piece of bread to start. So, our bottom slice is saying something positive about the staff member, something good. Don't lavish the praise, or it will seem false, turning him or her off. Use a transition statement like this one:

"David, there is something I want to share with you to help you improve something in your life. I say this to you kindly. I assure you that I value you as a member of our team. Would you kindly consider this?"

You will receive a nod of the head or a nervous "Okay" or a defensive "What's the problem?"

Smile warmly as you assure him you want to say something for his good or to help him grow in Christ. Then say it with kindness and meekness. (This is our mayonnaise or mustard being put on the slice of bread.)

One thing I have learned is that the word "kindly" breaks down barriers. I've used this word in fundraising with potential donors. "Would you kindly consider helping with Project X?" It helps set the person at ease, at least to some extent, and softens the blow.

After you have identified what you would like to see changed or done differently, tell him why but not in a way to attack him as a person. It helps to assure him again that you value him as a member of the team and you are not attacking him personally. Confront the problem rather than attack the person. (Now you have the slice of meat on your sandwich, maybe some cheese with it.)

After a short discussion, ask him for an agreement (see chapter called "It's Not Winning Arguments, It's Winning Agreements"). This can be phrased, "David, would you be kind enough to accept what I have shared with you and to do it as I am asking?" If the response is affirmative, then ask David if he understands. "So, from what I've said, what is your understanding of what we're talking about?" If there are problems, you will find out what they are by listening to David explain his understanding of the conversation. You may need more explanation. If he parrots it back to you in understandable fashion and his attitude seems good, then we have taken care of the middle of the sandwich. (If all goes well, you now have your piece of lettuce or slice of tomato on the sandwich.)

Now, let's finish the sandwich with the top piece of bread—praise and affirmation. Let's admit it, who likes to be criticized or confronted? Proverbs teaches that a wise person will accept discipline, criticism, or a performance evaluation. Seems to me that the best way to teach this is for me to be responsive in a positive way when someone with authority over me confronts me. If you or I respond the right way to this in our own lives, then those in our care will be influenced in a proper way.

Thank David for his positive response and give heartfelt appreciation for him as a person. Tell him that you have been blessed by his good response. If he struggled for a while, tell him you noted the change in him when he finally accepted your suggestion. It will strengthen your relationship with him and build him up rather than tear him down.

Ephesians 4:32 says, "And be ye kind one to another, tenderhearted, forgiving one another, even as God for Christ's sake hath forgiven you."

How to Do Fundraising

L earn to use the word "kindly."

Thanks for reading this chapter. I'm finished.

"What? There has to be more," you say. There is, but I want you to learn to use this important word when you ask people to fund your ministry or project.

Why? It sets the person at ease, at least to an extent. Takes the edge off. After all, the potential donor has a pretty good suspicion as to what you want. So do you want to battle resistance or set the person at ease?

Ask for an appointment. Fearful? Meeting someone in his or her office usually requires getting past the gatekeeper, that is, the personal assistant or secretary. They are trained to guard the boss. "And, may I ask, what is it that you wish to speak to him about?" The dreaded question. Let's back up. Be friendly on the phone with the gatekeeper. Be nice. "Hello! And, whom am I speaking with?" (This is what you ask, and suddenly you take charge of the phone call). "Jessica, oh, I have a special person in my life named Jessica. I love your name. How are you today?" (You're off to a better start. Keep going and you can hear the difference in her voice when she responds.) The secretary has a ton of pressure on her, and you are only one of many phone calls. It pays to be nice and care about what is on her shoulders. When the dreaded question comes, I like to say, "I know Mr. X is a busy man, and I am asking for ten minutes or so to ask for his advice and input. Would you mind if I wait to share what my project is until I see him? Would you be so kind?" If you have been very nice, giving a sincere compliment or had empathy, if the secretary admitted that today is a rough day, well, you probably have unlocked the gate.

In-person requests are much easier, such as catching a business leader before or after church, asking for a few minutes of his time. If he asks what it is about, tell him that you want his advice and input, but you would rather wait to share this with him in his office or at Starbucks for coffee. One man I talked with insisted on knowing what I wanted to talk about. His chin was rigid, his jaw set as he stood as tall as he could. "I kindly ask you to partner with me to win Hungary for Christ. Make an impact upon the young people. You send, I go. I kindly ask you to write a check for $25,000 for our meeting room renovation project so we can have a suitable place to preach the Gospel. Would you like to write the check right now?" Pretty bold. He liked that I would not be intimidated. He asked me to come to his office to talk this over. He wrote a check for an amount less than what I asked for, but it was still five figures. The apostle James says, "Ye have not, because ye ask not."

When you get into the office, look this person directly in the eye, giving a firm handshake with a warm smile on your face. Take a quick sweep around the room with your eyes, noting family pictures, favorite hobbies, motivational quotes, or whatever. "Nice office! Love the picture of your family. What a beautiful family!" He will probably tell you one or two are already grown, in college, or graduated from college and what line of work they are in. Two or three warm comments about his interests are very appropriate.

Then get to the point. Don't hem-haw around, acting like you're scared of your own shadow. Spit it out. Make eye contact, leaning forward just a bit in your seat. Give a mini-report of how the mission is doing or a quick story about a young teenage boy or girl who made a life-changing decision. But don't ramble. Keep it short and to the point. Then say, "Mr. X, I'm here to ask for your advice and your input. God has put it on my heart to reach the youth of our nation. I am serving with a wonderful mission, joining a team of missionaries who are committed to make an impact on our nation. Would you be so kind to consider my support needs so that I can do what God has called me to do?"

Then wait. He may ask you a couple of questions such as how much do you need or how he can support you. He may just stare at you for five seconds before saying anything. Don't flinch. Smile warmly and keep your eyes looking directly into his eyes.

Don't use the approach of asking them to pray for you, never getting around to asking for support. You can ask for their prayers *after* you ask for support. They may tell you, "No, not now." Or, "I am overloaded at the present time. I cannot do this." If so, tell them that you will check back at another time. Ask if you can count on them to pray for you. Ask for some prayer requests from them. Then, when you check back, you can comment about their prayer requests that you have been praying for, asking how things are going regarding these requests. This builds relationships.

We have not, because we ask not. Ask! Ask and you shall receive. Ever heard of these Bible verses? Sure you have. So do it! Do you want to be a missionary or not? Do you want to be married and have a family? Ask! Believe in yourself and be positive. You will eventually get results. Keep asking.

I will end with the beginning. Here is what you should do first:

Make a list of your family members, close friends, former teachers, influential people who you know, people in the past who made a positive impression upon your life, business leaders that you know, pastors of churches that are mission minded, and so on. Come up with fifty to one hundred names. Then contact them like I've taught you in this lesson. God bless you! Go get 'em!

How to Handle an Impossible Situation

The year 1996 held giant tests for me. One of them was the purchase of the famous Andrassy Castle in Toalmas, Hungary, where our mission was located on seventy-eight beautiful wooded acres.

God moved behind the scenes to bring about a lease of this property in July 1989. God used some great men to make all of this possible, such as Paul Bubar, Geza Kovacs Sr., Chuck Kosman, Harry Bollback, and Jack Wyrtzen. Others were involved at various levels, and I am thankful for each person's role. It was a privilege for me to be in attendance during the negotiations. I remember the night before we signed the lease agreement. Most of the Hungarian board members could not imagine that the trade union, who controlled the property, would actually give us a lease agreement. The mood during this board meeting was somber, with each of us praying to God for His help to make all of this possible.

God gave me something to say during the meeting at a critical time. "Can you imagine that the trade union officials are together in one of their homes having a similar meeting? Could it be that this is hard for them to believe as well? They may be wondering if our American organization is really sincere about this lease. After all, we will have to spend $50,000 just to build a new sewage system for the government to allow us to use the castle and the other thirteen buildings on the property."

One of the Hungarians agreed that the trade union people just might be meeting right at the time of our meeting. It seemed to help all of us move forward—by faith.

The next day, we signed the ten-year lease agreement, and we were praising God. After all, Hungary was still under the control of the Communists at that time. We had no idea that the Berlin wall would come down later in 1989. But God put us there on a miracle basis and at the right time to get us in. We had been approved by the government to begin our work with young people. It was a special moment.

For the next six years, I was negotiating for an extension of our ten-year lease agreement. I knew the time would pass rapidly, and we needed a longer agreement. The president of the trade union told me, at the end of our meeting in 1989, to come back to him after our first summer youth camp season and he would give us another lease. But he died before we had finished our first seven weeks of camp in 1990.

The control of the castle and our lease agreement changed hands three times. I had to start anew with each group that gained control. God gave me favor with each new leader. Each time, the new leader told me he was thankful for what I was doing in Hungary and that it was good for the Hungarian young people. Still, no lease extension or new lease. I chased this matter all the way to the prime minister's office, only to find that his undersecretary said that even the prime minister did not have the competency to sign an agreement with us, although he was grateful for our work.

In 1995, one of our supporters offered to buy the castle. We could hardly believe our ears when he made known his desire. The first bank transfer of his donation arrived in late 1995, and he wanted to make the second donation in the new calendar year, 1996, in order to have a tax receipt for both years. This seemed reasonable, and we agreed. But a new law came onto the books in Hungary on January 1, 1996. Our castle property had historical and environmental protection. Such properties would now be offered to the local government for the first opportunity or refusal to buy. Of course, the town government of Toalmas wanted the coveted property.

Life became a nightmare—dark, dark days. We had to wait to see the intentions of the township. We checked with a sister city in Germany that had a relationship with our small town. Sure enough, our town officials were trying to raise money from the Germans to buy the castle. The nightmare continued. Many prayers went before the Lord, asking for His help. I made one trip after another into Budapest to meet with lawyers, along with my assistant, Ildiko Barbarics, who was a legal counselor as well as one of our staff members. She was a great blessing.

Finally, one night I was sitting on the edge of the bed, and I said something aloud. "God, you gave this castle to us on a miracle basis, and the miracle is not over. Somehow, some way, and I don't know how it is going to happen, but you are going to work this out. I'm exhausted. I'm tired of trying to work it out myself. I turn it over to you, and I'm going to bed. I need some sleep."

Peace. I had a new sense of peace. I called my boss in New York and told him. There was silence on the line for a few seconds. Finally, he said he hoped and prayed that I was right. I was a different man from that day forward. I had agonized, worried, answered questions from nervous and worried staff members … you name it. Yes, I had been praying, but I was trying to fix things, find a solution, work on it, determined with a capital D that we would win. When I gave it to the Lord, He rewarded me with peace.

No, it was not solved immediately, as we had to wait through two thirty-day cooling-off periods that the local townspeople could protest or sound off. Wait, wait, wait, but I had peace in my heart. What had happened in my heart? I trusted God, and it was blind trust, because it did not look like it was going to work out favorably for us. I had been making plans for an alternative location in case we lost the castle property. I was a mess until I gave it to God. What a difference that night! I slept so well instead of tossing and turning. I was refreshed the next morning.

After these two cooling-off periods, my assistant, Ildiko, told me that we finally had the castle and could purchase it. I kept that choice news to myself for thirty more days. Why? I was waiting to see if another big "tree" would fall on our path, like another cooling-off period. I can't remember exactly, but I may have waited forty-five to sixty days before I made the big announcement. Where was my faith? Well, we had so many things go wrong during that time I was leery of something else happening to us. Sorry, but that's what I did. I waited before I said anything. Deep inside of me, I was praising God for His provision.

Trusting God was a big lesson for me. I am thankful for this difficult, trying experience. I learned so much about God. I felt like I had lived through an impossible situation. Certainly, the message from Luke 1:37 is that "For with God nothing shall be impossible."

How to Lead a Meeting

Every meeting starts fifteen minutes before it begins.

For example, a youth meeting should have background music playing in the room fifteen minutes before the meeting starts. All chairs should be in place. The bulletin board refreshed with a new youth article or updated calendar. Props ready to use for games, skits, or for the teaching time—everything ready to go fifteen minutes before the meeting starts. And one or two leaders at the door, ready to greet the young people as they come in.

Want to know why? You are setting the atmosphere. You want to build excitement that you are going to have a great meeting today, so you do these things ahead of time. When I ran youth camps in Hungary, I had staffers at the doors, keeping them closed until a few minutes before the meeting started. Music was pumping through the sound system, and they could hear it outside. A staff member was at each door greeting the kids, laughing and talking with them. There was such an air of excitement and anticipation being created outside, even before they came in. Yes, when we had rain, we had to let them in so they would not be soaked. Otherwise, when the doors opened, everyone ran in scrambling to get the prime seats. They were revved up!

Let's go to the part of the meeting when the speaker is about to give his message. Want the young people to be alert, ready to listen? Or is it okay if they are slumped in their seats, bored to death? I think you know the answer. So, how do you get them really ready for the speaker? Start the meeting fifteen minutes before it begins. That's how. Well, that's not all.

Some youth meetings start with the lights out, no music playing, with the gang dragging their feet on the floor, sitting on the middle of their spines slumped down in their seats, slowly exhaling their boredom and disgust. Then the youth leaders arrive, turning the lights on. Good grief! Discipline problems start as one boy shoves another, telling him to sit somewhere else. And you want to speak to this group with this mood? Come on!

Fast songs first. Why? Think of it this way—you are working hard to get the interest of the youth. Fast songs boost their enthusiasm. Get them up, up, up and on their feet! "Everyone, up, up, up! And I mean everyone! Let's go!" The sound guy starts the music or your band cranks it up. (Hey, have the band ready to go, on time. Not the lead singer trying to get his guitar in tune while everyone stands there in dead silence, waiting for the dork to get his act together.) Intro, hands clapping and varoom, you're singing a fast song with motions or hand clapping. Guess what? The group loves this! They absolutely eat it up! Then another fast one before you seat them.

For years I have used a funny skit, not a drama, not something of a serious nature, right in the middle of the song time. One or two fast songs, then something acted out that has them laughing their heads off. Slapstick, crazy, funny but not too long. Immediately get them back up on their feet with another song, somewhat fast. Medium fast. Pause to pray to God, asking Him to bless the meeting and speak to our hearts. Then a quick testimony, three minutes max. Someone who has had a dramatic change in his or her life. Next, a couple of slower songs to worship God. If you have the staffing to have soloists or a small group, do this right before the speaker is introduced.

Introducing the speaker is critical. You don't want to tear them down or make fun of them. "Hey, gang, tonight we are so privileged to have my friend and soon to be your friend. He has an awesome message that I cannot wait for all of us to hear. With great pleasure, I introduce to you _____. Put your hands together to welcome him!" Wow! That's a great buildup. You've just set your speaker on a pedestal, giving him the respect of your audience. He will be off to a running start as a result.

Back up. Let's back up to explain why to do all of this. Obviously, you are having the youth meeting to accomplish something very important. So, you work hard to capture the interest of the young people. Maybe there will be an invitation for them to receive Christ. Ultra important! Or you are having a meeting that will teach something or disciple the youth.

Think with me. Let's draw a perpendicular line, up and down, calling this the level of interest. Number it from zero to ten. Zero interest is snooze city, boring. One is very mild interest. Six or seven is very strong (laughing, cheering, or they are really sitting up in their seats, totally focused on the speaker and his message). Eight is incredible. We rarely make it to ten—that's a very, very special moment. Actually, you can hit a nine or ten with all of the campers coming forward at a campfire meeting dedicating their lives to the Lord. Ultra special! I live for those special moments. How about you?

Wait, there is another line, horizontal, connecting to the bottom of the perpendicular line (up and down). It represents time. Time from the start of the meeting (or, fifteen minutes before the meeting starts) until the conclusion, the end of the meeting. If you start the meeting in a boring way, the interest level is either zero or minus three in some cases. Ugh! Juice it up, as I described earlier, and you just might be starting at two or three. What you are trying to do is get the crowd ready for the speaker. You don't want the interest level to be at one or two or less when he gets up to speak. Groan! This puts the speaker in a tough spot. Let's think of God being at work in all of this, with a right philosophy of leading meetings. God will bless the preaching no matter what. But if we can create an exciting atmosphere, we can have the crowd ready to listen, more attentive. By the way, these methods work with senior adults. Surprised? It's true because people prefer a meeting with life to it.

So, faster songs increase the interest level, raising it to a four maybe. Five? Great! A silly, crazy, funny skit keeps it there. Then we are going to minister to the heart with praise music, a great testimony, and special music that could be slow, medium, or fast. I always tell the soloist what type of song I want to fit the meeting. The first night of youth camp, it should be faster. The second night it can be slower. So, the interest level goes up and down during the twenty-five to thirty minutes before the speaker is on stage. That's okay. We cannot keep the youth so stoked they are screaming their lungs out when it is time to pray. There are natural ups and downs in the interest level throughout the meeting.

Your speaker is seeking God's direction regarding his message. Your job is to set the stage, giving him a group of excited young people eager to listen to God's Word.

How to end the meeting? Depends upon the theme of the meeting. Evangelism, discipleship meeting, campfire meeting, banquet—plan out what you are going to say to end the meeting. Put some time and effort into this. What will you say? Anything you need to prepare before the meeting? End the meeting with class. This will not happen if you do not put time into your preparation, not just for the beginning of the meeting but the conclusion as well.

Extra note: If you are leading weekly youth meetings in a church, I urge you to do a preview of next week's meeting at the conclusion of this week's meeting. Use various methods for this promo, such as a short skit acting out some scene from the next meeting or a printed handout (use your creativity)—something to get the interest level up regarding the next meeting.

Extra note: If you are inexperienced at leading meetings, practice in front of a mirror at home. I am serious. Yes, I did this years ago. Practice makes perfect.

How to Mentor

Big subject—can't cover it all in a single chapter. But let's get started.

Jot down what your mentors taught you in the past. Keep a notepad with you to jot down more ideas as subjects or experiences come back to you. Aren't you grateful for what someone imparted to you? Tell the Lord how thankful you are.

A second list is necessary because you will think of things you wish they had taught you. You've learned those things the hard way, yet they are jewels. Now you have a pretty good start. Just in case, here are some basics to cover:

How to have a quiet time. How to study the Bible. Which books of the Bible are critical to your mentee. One chapter from Proverbs every day. How to pray. Verses to memorize. How to witness. Tithing and giving. How to know God's will. Teach him or her to train and disciple others (2 Tim. 2:2). Thankfulness. Teachable spirit—and more

And the list continues, as this is just a start—a good start.

Be simple and teach how. Be honest regarding your failures in any of these areas or what you learned the hard way. Your openness regarding failure will help so, so much. Now that they know you are a real person, they begin to learn that failure can become a stepping-stone to success. It gives them hope and takes the pressure off your younger disciples.

You simply cannot teach what you have not experienced yourself. If you try, they will see right through you and not respect you. So put some time in on these subjects to prepare yourself. Truth is you only have to be a few steps ahead of your mentees. But you need to keep digging for yourself to stay ahead of them. As a result, you will inspire them when you tell them that you have not learned it all and are still learning.

When you invest the time and effort, you will be rewarded with a disciple who is developing a hunger to learn more. You will be blessed beyond measure and begin to look forward to your weekly meetings with enthusiasm.

Don't lose heart if your young disciple wants to drop out. Of course, you will make an effort to encourage them to continue. If they refuse, keep in mind that God promises in Isaiah 55:11 that His Word will not return void but will accomplish what He pleases, and it will prosper in the way that He sends it. This is a huge promise! Your time is not in vain because God is still at work (see the chapter called "God Is at Work"). What do you do? Find someone else and get started again. Your labor is not in vain (1 Cor. 15:58).

How to Speak

Dale Carnegie has a book and a course on how to speak in public. It would be a good idea to pick up a copy and read it through. Over the years, I have given countless speeches, taught lessons, given seminars, led public meetings, and preached. Some people would die of fright if they had to speak in public or in church. Others are just getting started with their careers and need to learn more about how to speak.

Start with a personal humorous experience to let the audience get to know you and become comfortable with you.

Most speeches have three points. Some have more, but be careful to limit your number of points. Personally, I give one-point messages when I speak. One point to get across to the people in attendance. I use one or two stories to amplify the point.

Stories? Yes, they are like word pictures, painting a portrait. A story explains the point that you are trying to make, and the audience can better remember your point by connecting the topic with your story. People love stories. See the chapter called "Become a Storyteller." I get my stories from the Bible, telling what a biblical character did. Or I use personal experiences because people like real-life stories. You know your own stories better than anyone else. Think through experiences as a child or when you were a teenager or in your adult life. Which one could apply to the main point or points that you are speaking on?

Eye contact, eye contact, eye contact—sweep the audience on the right, not fast, looking into their eyes. Move to the left, making eye contact with this person, then that person. Move to the center and do the same. Go back to the left side and pick one face, one person, and linger there looking at him or her, while continuing to speak. It's as though you are talking just to one person, yet everyone else gets to listen. Then swing over to the right side and do the same. Why? People's minds can drift away if you do not look at them. Back to the center of the audience, then back to the right side. It helps keep their attention. This takes the edge off of the fear of speaking to the whole group.

Fear? If this is an issue for you, try deep breathing before you start. And prayer. Ask God to help you communicate what He wants to be told. When I speak to teenagers or children, I get so fired up or revved up, as I call it. Young people love enthusiasm. They want someone to follow. If you are boring, they will turn you off so fast, and their minds will be miles away. This is how God wired me. For someone who has never done this before, it may feel like a daunting task, but I'm confident you can do it. Read on for some suggestions to help you.

Are you more of an introverted person? If so, you need to think through what you will say before you say it. You probably need a script with every word written. This will require considerable practice, giving your speech to an imaginary audience, talking aloud. However, don't keep your nose glued to the script when you speak in public. You will come across as boring. You must know some of your material so well that you can look at people long enough to quote from memory two or three sentences. Mark or highlight your notes or outline to help you quickly find your next point. Needless to say, practice much.

Learn to slow down, using voice inflection at a rate to give emphasis and importance to a valuable point in your speech or message. The attention level of the audience will increase because of this.

Lastly, practice in front of a mirror. I did years ago. It works because you see the expression on your face, making changes to get the expression that you want to have. Practice slowing down, watching your face as you speak more slowly, emphasizing your main point. Practice voice inflection, watching your face become more serious. By voice inflection, I mean the deepening of your voice, slowly pronouncing your words for emphasis. Or you make your voice somewhat stronger as you state your key point. The tendency is to talk fast because you are nervous. What I am teaching you helps you deal with this.

Oh yes, I hope you can do this in privacy so they don't come to lock you up in the insane asylum. Just joking. Practice, practice, practice. Pray, pray, pray. Then get out there and do it! May God bless you as a speaker.

If There Is a Will, God Will Find a Way

Feeling a burden for Montenegro, God led me to travel there for some exploratory trips in 2006–07. Finding only three evangelical churches in the country at that time, I soon began to realize there is a great need for evangelism, church planting, and the development of a youth camp.

Twelve people, ten men and two women, came to an information meeting that I conducted. During the meeting, I learned that there were only about 120 believers in the country at that time. Doing the math in my mind, I was stunned that I had 10 percent of the total amount of Christians in Montenegro sitting in this meeting. "How many Christian young people are there in the country?" I queried. "Oh, eight or nine, at least," answered one of the pastors. Not eighty-nine. Eight or nine. As I thought about it, I knew that I could not depend upon the teenagers to bring enough friends to fill up the camp. No four-color brochure with a mass mailing. I had to find the potential campers. Whew!

Not only that, they were not ready for the youth camp ministry philosophy that I was sharing. Believe it or not, one man suggested that I go back to Budapest to my home. "These ideas will not work here," he said with an authoritative tone of finality.

After a couple of days, that is exactly what I did—I returned to Hungary where I lived. In a few days, one of the pastors called apologizing. "I am so sorry. My people are not ready for what you were sharing. Please do not be offended. What about doing this as a day camp?"

Despite my mind screaming at me, "I've never done it this way before," I decided to give it a try, agreeing to return to make some plans.

Walking around Niksic, Montenegro, the second largest city, I found a basketball court/soccer field lit up at night with lights. Sixty to seventy young people of various ages were hanging out. The big boys were playing basketball, dominating the action while I worked the sidelines talking to all of the kids to see who spoke English. Praying, I continued to go there each night. Can you believe that at age fifty-seven, I played basketball, hanging out with these youth, building relationships? Ever heard of the designated hitter in baseball? Well, I think I invented the designated foul in basketball. Oh my, I could not keep up with these young guys, but I could slow them down with illegal blocks and hacking my way to rebounds. The whole time, I was jabbering away in English trying to connect with whoever was listening.

Finally, one night after the big guys finished an exhausting game, I walked out onto the court yelling, "Hi, everybody! My name is Eric. Come here if you speak English! Let's go! Move it! Now, now, now! Move, move, move!" About thirty shuffled over as I told them about Camp Monty. We planned to teach English and basketball as well as tell them about God and that He loves them. As long as I could keep talking, they hung around to listen.

Each night I "played" basketball and talked up a storm. Then I announced that we would start Camp Monty the next day. It just so happened that two parents showed up about that time yelling at me. A young fifteen-year-old guy was translating for me until he became frightened. I had no idea what these parents were saying, so I put my hands behind my back and stood there with a smile. I could tell they were really upset about something, but I had no idea what the problem was. One stopped yelling at me, so the other one spit on us. My granddaughter was close to me at the time, and she received most of the spittle. Oh me.

Finally, they ran out of steam and walked away shouting at the young people. One of the boys I had talked with earlier asked me if I would be coming back the next night. Well, yes, this was the group of youth that I had been concentrating on. I planned to come back. He said, "Good. I will watch you be killed." Say what? The Montenegrin youth drew closer to see what I would do or say. He asked if I understood what the parents had said, and I told him that I did not understand the language. So, he told me what they said, explaining that they were just yelling and nothing would happen. Oh really?

Can you imagine how I felt as I walked back to the pastor's home where I was staying? "Oh, God, I know you put it on my heart to come to Montenegro. What is happening? What do I do? I *have* to go back there tomorrow night because I need to continue to build relationships, trying to get these young people to come to Camp Monty. Help me, Lord!"

Guess how many campers we had on our first day of camp? One. We had twenty-eight workers there, Americans, Romanians, and Hungarians. One camper! I rallied the troops at the basketball gym for the basketball instruction next morning. "Spread out on the court for exercises! We need to make it look like we have a crowd here!" The workers were so, so responsive, showing much enthusiasm trying to encourage me.

The second day we had two campers. With a burst of enthusiasm, I thrust my hand upwards. "A 100 percent increase! Yay!"

My translator somberly said, "Eric, we have *two* campers. Just two." True, but I was pumped!

Day three we had seven, and I was almost out of my gourd. On the fourth day, we had nineteen, and I gave the Gospel message. Guess who received Christ that day? The seventeen-year-old boy who said he would watch me be killed if I came back. Suddenly, the adversity started making sense to me! God used the threats and my calm reaction to get the attention of these young people. This was the catalyst for change! God turned the negative into a positive!

On the final day of Camp Monty 2007, we had thirty-two campers. Finally, more campers than workers! Hallelujah!

The last few years, we have had more than four hundred teens attending the one-week session of Camp Monty each summer. Amazing!

By the way, I went back to that outdoor sports complex the next night—no one came to kill me. They had said that if I came back, they would use axes to kill me. God protected me.

God will test you, try you. How will you react?

P.S. By the third summer, on the last day of Camp Monty, parents lined up to thank me for coming to Montenegro. They shook my hand or hugged me or kissed me. Only God can make something like this happen!

It's Lonely at the Top

When I was a boy, we played a game called King of the Hill. The point was to push all of the other boys down the hill while maintaining your position on top of the hill. It was a typical rough-and-tumble boys' game. Shove the other boy back down the hill while looking for another boy making his way to the top. Try to wear the other boys out as they tumbled head over heels down the hill. Sometimes three of the boys would mount an attack to grab the king of the hill by his ankles to pull him down. If successful, those three would wrestle each other to become the new king of the hill.

The business world is full of young executives who aspire to get to the top. They think they can do a better job, if only the big boss would retire or step aside. Some of them make it to the top of the hill, the king of the hill, only to find that it is very lonely at the top.

It is no different for Christian leaders. The pastor learns he can't share his deepest, innermost thoughts with another man in his congregation. He can talk about his goals of building up and growing the church, but he has to be careful to keep up a front to guard himself. He fears that he can't tell everything that is in his heart. After a few years, he realizes life at the top is very, very lonely. He wants to find a friend or two to share his heart.

It was lonely in the garden …

Jesus was in the garden of Gethsemane praying. He knew what was coming next—betrayal, trial, and crucifixion. He asked the disciples if they would pray with Him, but they became sleepy, leaving Him all alone at a difficult time in His life. Lonely, very lonely.

What does a leader do when he is so lonely at the top? Jesus went to God the Father in prayer. The leader *has* to develop his personal devotional life or he will come apart because of all the pressure being at the top. It's not a little boys' game anymore, when everyone decides to go get some ice cream or play a different game. It's real life. You have to learn how to feed yourself.

Spending time with God in prayer, pouring out your heart to Him, satisfies the needs deep inside of you. God desires to have a relationship with you, meeting with you early in the morning and throughout the day as you speak to the Almighty in sentence prayers, thanking Him for His help. God has brought you to this place to deepen the relationship. Indeed, He is closer than a brother, as the scripture states. Talk to God; pour your heart out. Then praise Him just like King David showed us in Psalms. In many of the psalms, David takes his problems to God—his frustrations—his battles—his despair. But he concludes every psalm with praise to God. This is the pattern, the example. So do this in your loneliness. He is waiting for you.

It's Not Winning Arguments,
It's Winning Agreements

When I was much younger, working with some leaders close to my age, we would argue. Not all the time, just sometimes. It seemed that we were honing our skills to debate. Thinking about this later, I think I was learning to destroy rather than debate. Yes, I have some regrets about this.

In my late thirties, I was slowly coming to a new way of thinking. Better to win agreements rather than win arguments. In my forties, this was becoming more refined in my thinking. I'm not saying I was perfect in this, but I was growing and changing. I felt better about myself and began to treat the other person better.

One thing that helped me is that I learned to wait for more information. Too many rash decisions earlier because I did not have full information. How many times did I say, "Oh, if I would have known, I would not have made this decision." More information. In my early thirties, I picked this bit of information up in a book on sales by Frank Bettger. When negotiating or trying to find out what reason is making the buyer delay his purchase or not purchase, ask the following question. "In addition to this, is there anything else?" Simple question, but it gets results. Ask this question and wait for an answer. What you will hear next may surprise you, or it may be the sticking point as to why you cannot come to an agreement. All you have to do is to answer or satisfy the other person after he tells you this.

"In addition to this, is there anything else?" could be the solution to winning an agreement. Winning an argument leaves a bad taste in the other person's mouth—in his memory. You will have great difficulty the next time you argue, uh, excuse me, negotiate.

What's the point? Does your ego really need to win this badly? Do you need to destroy in order to pamper your ego?

Keep your cool and go for win-win victories. Make it a win for the other person and a win for you. It *can* be done. When listening to the other person, instead of thinking how inane their arguments are—how silly, how dumb—try looking at the negotiation from their point of view. What can you do to make them happy or solve their problem? What can you give that will cause the other person to modify or give? What difficulties might he or she be having in his or her life right now? How can I show empathy and care? Pray for God's wisdom that you can come up with a solution that is not necessarily fifty-fifty but a win-win, putting a smile on the other person's face. This will make for a pleasant discussion or negotiation in the future with this person. Winning agreements has been a game changer for me. I hope that you will agree because it will work for you also.

John 6:66

Whoa—666? Spooky numbers, right?

The scenario in the latter part of John, chapter 6 shows us a very lonely, difficult moment for Jesus in His earthly ministry. "From that time many of his disciples went back, and walked no more with him" (John 6:66).

It is a very lonely moment for a leader when people leave him. Staff members, workers, volunteers. Speaking from experience, I can tell you it hurts. It is painful.

In fact, Jesus asks a question of the twelve disciples in verse 67. "Then said Jesus unto the twelve, Will ye also go away?" Can you feel the loneliness?

One time a staff member told me, "I feel like we are two ships passing in the night." I realized if he was not on my ship, he needed to sail on. I had worked hard trying to keep him on the team only to realize when someone wanted to go, I should let him go. I had spun my wheels in vain.

If you are a leader, you are going to experience the agony of team members leaving you. Keep in mind that even Jesus Himself experienced this. This is no small statement, my friend. Jesus knows your pain because He went through this. He was in human flesh with the same feelings you and I have. Take solace in this fact—it happened to Jesus. It will happen to you. Maybe it already has.

Okay, don't dwell on this. Don't let it get you down. It's our tendency to blame ourselves, or we wonder what is wrong with us. Good grief, this happened to Jesus.

What do we do? Keep moving forward. God may have protected you. Or He may be leading the other person to a new ministry. Let's not question God. We may never understand. Just keep moving forward because there are others on the team who need you, and they need you to be at your best.

Pray the following: "Dear God, so and so just left me. This hurts so bad, and I need You to help me with this. Give me grace to bear this. I pray for the other person. Help him/her, guide him/her. I do not want to be resentful. I want the best for this person. Lord, I need to keep moving forward, but I cannot do it without Your help. Help me. I praise You for Your faithfulness and Your help. I love you, God. I praise You."

Joshua Needed Another Joshua

Moses had Joshua. Paul had Timothy. Elijah had Elisha.

But Joshua did not have another Joshua. Ouch!

Joshua was Moses's right-hand man through thick and thin. Joshua had witnessed Moses handle so many difficulties with God's help. He waited for Moses when the Ten Commandments were given. He was a faithful second man, playing a vital role for Moses. Joshua was a star witness of every miracle, from the Red Sea to the parting of the waters again, crossing a swollen Jordan River.

I have wondered how Joshua must have felt when he learned of Moses's death. Loneliness. Fear. Uncertainty. Then God spoke to Joshua, telling him to be of good courage and not to fear. Just as He had been with Moses, He would be with Joshua. Read all of Joshua, chapter 1 to get the feel of what happened. Joshua immediately did what God commanded.

As I search the book of Joshua, I cannot find where there was another young Joshua, another young leader that was discipled. Finally, in chapters 23 and 24, Joshua is very old and gives final commandments to the tribal leaders, the same words that God had said to Joshua in chapter 1. Joshua was faithful to the Lord until the end of his life.

Next, we go to Judges, chapter 1 to see what happened after Joshua's death. Judah comes to the forefront after the leaders prayed to God. God answered, telling what Judah should do. Judges continues on, noting the success and failures of the tribes who did not fully obey God to drive out the inhabitants. There was no true leader, no Moses, no Joshua. Joshua had not used the important principle of discipling young leaders. He was faithful in all that God told him to do, but Joshua must not have thought about who would follow him in leadership as he had followed Moses.

In 2 Timothy 2:2 is a vital principle, as Paul taught us. Who are you discipling? Who are you teaching what God has taught you through those who helped you when you were young? Give this your utmost attention.

Over the years, I have had a friend or two about ten years older than me and a couple of friends ten to fifteen years younger than me. I have had some mentors twenty to forty years older than me. I have learned from all of them. Having a couple of friends older than me gives me examples to watch as I age, seeing how they handle the aging process. To those who are younger than me, I realize that I play this role for them. Yet I look beyond this to find a young man or two to invest my life in. I pray about this, asking God to give me wisdom to fulfill 2 Timothy 2:2 with younger men who could take my place at some point in the future.

This is vitally important. I encourage you to invest quality time in this form of discipleship. So, who is your Joshua? Your Timothy? Your Elisha? All you have to do is to read the pitiful report in the book of Judges to realize how important this is. Get going on this today, not tomorrow. Today.

Keep the Romance Alive

Remember the first time that you met her? Or for the ladies reading this—that you met him? Special memory, right? Want to keep the romance alive and growing? I do! Why not?

Words—so precious. Words can build up, encourage, motivate, and express our feelings. Tell her often that you love her. How often? More than once a day! She never tires of hearing these special words from you, "I love you."

Use Post-it Notes, putting them in places where she will see them again and again—inside a kitchen cabinet, on her mirror, on the steering wheel in the car. Write a love note and mail it to her. Write another one, placing it in her lingerie drawer. Buy her favorite flowers, not just on her birthday. What woman does not like chocolate? Gentle foot rubs turn into gentle back rubs that turn into, well, you know what they turn into.

Don't be like the fellow who stopped telling his wife that he loved her. After several months of marriage, his wife was crying that he never tells her he loves her. "I told you that I love you the day we were married. If anything changes, I'll let you know." Ugh!

You be the energizer. *You* take the initiative, sir. I will tell you that she *will* respond in kind. Romance her until the casket, whoever goes first.

Be creative. Think of ideas to express your love. Start off with these suggestions. Take walks holding hands. Tell her how much she means to you and how much you love her. Come up with your phrases to use, such as, "I'm totally crazy about you. I thank God for you. I'm so glad that God brought us together. I'm excited about you. You turn me on. I love hanging out with you. I like to cuddle with you. You are the best. You are awesome and incredible—the best wife in the world. I love you to the moon and back. You make my day. You make me complete. You are exactly what I need. I'm so thankful for you. You make me happy." That's only a start.

Listen to her. Ask her about her day and then really listen. Ask questions about her feelings. At other times, make her feel like she is part of your life by asking her for her input regarding some situation you are going through. Thank her for her suggestions and use them when you can.

Have daily Bible reading and devotions together. I cannot emphasize how important this is to your wife. She has a hunger for this, and it is your responsibility to meet this need. Pray together. You lead this prayer time but also ask her to lead in prayer sometimes. Some couples alternate praying aloud. Hold hands while praying or try to be as close together as possible. Sometimes pray before or after sex—it is a deeply spiritual experience for both of you. After all, sex is God's gift for husbands and wives. Why not thank Him for this precious gift?

Speaking of sex—if you will meet her needs first, most of the time, you will have a very satisfied wife who will bring you to even more romantic and fulfilling sexual expressions of your love for each other. I have shared a very important secret with you. You will be glad, and she will be appreciative beyond measure.

Leading Music

Music in youth camps and in churches has evolved over the years. When I was a child, I remember music with a march tempo that was probably influenced by music written to rouse Americans to support the war effort during World War II. Then we had a wave of folk music that was influenced by the hippy movement in the States, folk music with Christian words and themes. That along with peppy, fun songs similar to the ones that I brought to Hungary when I started a youth camp there in 1990. They fit with my personality. I would sing fast songs at the beginning of the meeting, using a philosophy that prepared the hearts of the young people for the message—asking the youth to stand up and do motions with certain songs. There would be an air of excitement and anticipation of having a very special meeting, expecting God to bless in a great way.

Blending in a zany, funny skit with camp program staff serving as actors, the young people would laugh heartily. Then another fast song followed by a rousing solo from one of the music staff would add excitement to the meeting. After a short testimony from a counselor or staff member, I began to sing slower songs that took us into worship, preparing us for the message. This philosophy worked very well. Extremely well.

Today's music is so different, with praise or worship songs that are slower for the most part. But they seem to connect with today's young people. I encourage using some faster praise songs at the beginning of the meeting, a skit or drama, a testimony, a solo followed by slower songs, then the message.

When you are starting out as a worship leader, you have to find your style, your personality. If you play the guitar, you can open the meeting by playing something fast on the guitar, just a few chords, that gets the attention of the young people. All guitar players have favorite chords, notes, or progressions that they like to play when relaxing or when practicing guitar. Then you greet everyone with enthusiasm, telling them we are going to have a wonderful time today in our meeting. "Hey, everyone, stand up and let's sing with everything that we have." Lifting your guitar up and moving toward the group, strum the guitar with gusto, repeating the special chords or notes that you played earlier. "Up, up, up! Everybody, up! Let's sing!" you call out as you play the introduction of the song.

If they don't sing out right at first, put your arms up, stopping the song. "Hey, hey, hey, you call this singing? This was almost terrible." Say it as you look down to the floor or up to the ceiling, rolling your eyes, pretending to be sad. It will get them laughing as you jokingly criticize their efforts. "Now, let me hear you *really* sing! Come on! Let's go! Back to the beginning!"

Change what you say as you start each meeting. Don't use the same phrases each time. For example, the next meeting you can start off with chords that you strum several times, raising the chord by one half step each time. Go up four half steps as though you are building up to a big crescendo, a big climax. It will bring the group to life! Finish it with a shout, "Ole" like the crowd at a bullfight, or a loud "Hey, hey, hey!" You are trying to establish your personality, your way of leading music. You have to do something to get the meeting going, to get the crowd excited. You play a critical role in preparing the group to hear the message, the Word of God. (See the chapter called "How to Lead Meetings.")

The songs that follow will go more smoothly, and the young people will enjoy the worship or praise music much better. It is very appropriate and worshipful to raise your hand to the Lord in certain slow praise songs. In doing this, you strum the chord at the beginning of the measure in the song that is meaningful. Several young people will join you in raising their hands. As you know, chords change throughout the song, so you will need to be ready to play the next chord change as you move your hands back to the guitar. Do this as you feel led by the Lord. In other words, do not do this to be theatrical. Only do this as an act of worship. The practical side of this is that you will need to change chords at certain times or the group will not be singing the right notes.

You will gain confidence and enjoy your important ministry of setting the stage for the preaching of the Gospel. Please remember that the most important part of the meeting is the preaching, so do everything that you can, as unto the Lord, to prepare for the message.

Let It Go!

We all have our doctrinal differences, some small, some significant. T D Jakes, a pastor in Houston, Texas, and televangelist, is one with whom I would have some doctrinal differences. But we can learn from many people in the ministry. Occasionally, I have listened to him talk about Bible answers for spiritual problems and enjoyed some of his teaching. I was counseling a couple of people when I was in Europe recently, and I read the article to them. Both wanted a copy. Both asked to read it for themselves after I read it aloud. Both found one or two topics or themes in the message that they needed to *let it go*! Guess what? I read it again every so often. I keep it with me and read it from time to time. The title is "The Battle is the Lord's!"

Here is one example in the message:

> There are people who can walk away from you. When people can walk away from you … let them walk. Your destiny is never tied to anybody that left. People leave you because they are not joined to you (I John 2:19). LET THEM GO!
>
> … And, it doesn't mean that they are a bad person - it just means that their part in the story is over. And you've got to know when people's part in your story has ended so that you don't keep trying to raise the dead. You've got to know when it's dead. LET THEM GO!
>
> If you are holding on to past hurts and pains … LET IT GO!
>
> If someone can't treat you right, love you back, and see your worth … LET IT GO!!
>
> If someone has angered you … LET IT GO!!!

If you're stuck in the past and God is trying to take you to a new level in Him … LET IT GO!!!!

If you're feeling depressed and stressed … LET IT GO!!!!!

If there is a particular situation that you are so used to handling yourself and God is saying "Take your hands off of it," then you need to … LET IT GO!!!!!!

Let the past be the past. Forget the former things. GOD is doing a new thing for you now. LET IT GO!!!!!!!(3)

Okay, it's me writing now—you know what? *I really like this.* I didn't copy the whole thing, choosing the parts that might be of help to you. I find that I have to go over this every now and then. I read it again as I take one or more sentences, thinking of some negative situation that I put into my hands … raise my hands as toward heaven—to the Lord—and open my hands as I proclaim (in my mind) "I let it go!"

Listen Up!

J ob 13:5 says, "O that ye would altogether hold your peace! And it should be your wisdom."

Job 13:13 says, "Hold your peace, let me alone, that I may speak, and let come on me what will."

How difficult is it to listen? How difficult is it to keep quiet for sixty seconds?

The editors of *Fortune* magazine polled the wives of some business executives and discovered that "listening to their husbands" was their number-one duty.

C.G. Trumbull has a thrilling chapter on how to win a hearing in his little book *Taking Men Alive*: "To be a good listener is one of the surest ways of winning and holding men. The 'I can help you' attitude is fatal in this work; the 'you are helping, or interesting to me' spirit is one of the secrets of working with men."(4)

Please be quiet and listen. Job considered it the highest of wisdom. Don't just sit back and listen, but sit up and listen. It is an active performance. Most men must be classified as half listeners. The three friends of Job listened just long enough to be polite, then started on their remedies trying to fix him.

Job, the one needing help, cries, "I have heard many such things. Miserable comforters are ye all" (Job 16:2). Unburdening is important. People have troubles. People have burdens. They just need to "unload" on a good listener.

Often you may be asked to offer advice or give solutions to the problem at hand. Or, your friend may not want your advice or counsel at all. They just want the opportunity to talk freely. They need to listen to their own thoughts as they are put into words.

This is the ministry of listening quietly and objectively—the highest wisdom! The art of being a sounding board. Not a cross examiner but soaking up their words like a sponge.

Don't sit in judgment, ready to pounce. To be a good listener, be shock proof—at least outwardly. "It is not listening in itself that is important; it is the attitude with which a man listens. Much harm can be done by 'ears' whose reactions to what they hear are negative …"(5)

By the way, if you are a person who realizes that you talk too much, dominating conversations, place your chin on your hand. That is, lean forward somewhat supporting your chin with your hand and your elbow on a table. Literally, you are keeping your mouth closed.

Listening can be a greater service than speaking. (Eye contact—nodding of the head—facial expressions—key questions.) This is vital in building up a staff. When someone realizes that you will listen to him or her completely unload a burden, he or she is more open to kind advice. They will give you loyalty and go the extra mile for you because you have gone the extra mile by taking time to listen and to care.

James 1:19 says, "Wherefore, my beloved brethren, let every man be swift to hear, slow to speak, slow to wrath."

Looking for Potential in People

Look for potential in guys—you will always have girls who want to be part of the mission, the team. Invest in young men; see their potential and tell them about it. "I can see you as a program director in camp. I can visualize you giving the invitation, preaching just like I do. I can see it happen someday." They will be energized by these statements. They need to know what you think about their future.

Or, "You know what I see you doing in the future? You will be leading the games, the activities. You are a natural-born leader because this is how God has gifted you. The kids will be laughing their heads off having a great time. I can see this potential in you." The young man will be both stunned and happy. Your words will be so encouraging to him.

Don't make these statements to just any young man. Ask God to guide you to sharp, young men who have a heart for God. Always be on the outlook for potential. Even at my age, when I am in various countries, I am looking for potential leaders. I have a section in my daily prayer list devoted to young men in whom I see great potential. I call out their names to God, asking Him to develop their potential.

Give them something to do, something that is not too demanding, and see how they handle this. You can always add more at a later time. Praise them when you see their accomplishments. We all hunger for praise because it helps us to know that we are doing what the leader wants. This is a great motivation for young leaders who are growing.

Feed them spiritually, sharing what you do on a daily basis. Give them bits of information rather than telling them everything you do because it will overwhelm them. Get them going in a daily quiet time. Teach them how to pray and pray with them. We get to know each other much better when we listen to each other pray. It shows the heart of a person. Keep sharing more of what you do to feed yourself, your spiritual habits. You will be able to tell which ones are going to stick and which ones will fall by the wayside.

There will be some boys who just do not get it. It hurts to see them go, but God may be protecting you so that you do not waste time. Jesus suffered some loss in John 6:66–67. After this, a lot of His disciples left. They no longer wanted to be associated with Him. Then Jesus gave the twelve their chance: "Do you also want to leave?" Tough time for our Lord.

Risking the ire of young ladies, I would like to point out that Jesus chose men when He called the twelve men to join Him. Yet Jesus was kind to Mary and Martha as well as other women. My point is that we should focus on seeing the potential in young men, asking them to join your team. The girls will follow, and you can give them plenty of ministry to do. We need young ladies on the team, and these young men will marry some of these wonderful young ladies. After some time, the young wives will bring the sweetest children into the world. They will be busy raising these precious children—for a long time. All of this is good. Maybe they will be raising up the next generation of leadership. Wonderful! Young ladies can serve for a period of time as single girls. But at some point they will get married, God willing. This will take them in a new direction. Some of them will marry men who are not part of the team. They will always be friends of the ministry. Those who marry men who are part of the team will be involved in a closer way, but they will be busy raising the children. It's a fact of life. It's not bad. It's just how it is.

Pray that God will show you just the right young men to pursue.

Make the Boss Look Good

Sound self-serving? Not really.

I learned this concept standing next to Harry Bollback, who was emceeing the rodeo at the Word of Life Ranch. The ranch is a special place for children, an incredible, first-class children's youth camp. Jack Wyrtzen was on his favorite horse, joining other riders playing a version of polo. Harry was on the microphone, building up the competition as no one else can do. Parents and children were loving the performance, cheering and clapping.

Looking at me (with the microphone off), Harry told me that he wanted to make the boss look good. The way he said the word "boss" was more like "The Boss!" As he continued to describe the competition and the movement of the riders, he waited for the moment for the ball to get close to The Boss. Then he declared The Boss as the winner, ending the competition as the audience applauded. It was fun.

"Good job, Harry. You honored Jack." I smiled.

"Eric, he's the Boss," he said, Harry's eyes boring into mine. I noted his coast-to-coast smile. I liked the moment. It was good.

I had the privilege of being with each of these great men on tour doing evangelism. One year with Jack and the next with Harry, and so forth, for nine years. It was a special privilege. I watched Jack when he telephoned Harry, noting the special love between these men. The same was true when I watched Harry speak to Jack on the phone. The special look on his face, his voice resonated deep respect and love for The Boss. It seemed to me that Harry always wanted to make The Boss look good. And you know what? Jack always wanted to make Harry look good. I overheard a number of conversations. Time and again I excused myself to slip away, but both Jack and Harry motioned for me to stay nearby.

They were teaching me, showing me what to do in building close relationships between the top leader and his key man.

Each man knew that the other had imperfections and shortcomings. We all do. Yet, they built each other up at every opportunity. I witnessed this in person again and again. It made an indelible impression upon me.

What am I talking about? Servant leadership. They never told me that this was the concept, but this is what they were modeling for me and for others. Servant leadership works two ways. The main leader serves those under him or her, pouring his or her life into them, making sacrifices for them. These leaders sense this love and commitment, honoring The Boss. It's not lording over people. This is wrong. The idea is to serve those in your care. This *is* the point.

Let's think about Jesus, the Son of God. He was a man when He was here on earth, yet He was God. What did Jesus do all of His earthly life? Could I suggest that He sought to make The Boss look good? How so? He did the will of the Father. He was obedient. He sacrificed His life because it was the will of the Father, the plan of God for mankind, for you and me.

Yes, I would say that Jesus is the best example of servant leadership. It's great to see this concept modeled for us through great leaders now in our lifetime. Truth is this is what God the Father wants you and me to do right now. Serving those in our care is a way to honor God. As a result, those who are in our care love us and desire to serve, which honors God.

Making Your Budget from Your Calendar

Before computers, our staff would prepare our annual budgets using forms that looked like modern spreadsheets. Using a chart with the first box on the left for the account line, twelve boxes left to right for the months of the year, and a box for the total at the far right, we worked on our plan for ministry.

Serving as the regional director overseeing this process for our team, I noticed that a couple of the men were somewhat bewildered, trying to figure out what amount to put down for fuel or postage and which month to use. We had already written down our estimated income from our supporters, honorariums for speaking, and from the youth events. The thought came to me (from the Lord) to go to the white board to show how to do this. I pulled out my calendar, and using my plan for ministry for a certain month as an example, I sketched a month on the board.

Using the first weekend, I estimated how much money I would need to spend to drive to a certain city where I planned to preach in a church. Emphasizing using as much of the weekend as possible for ministry, I told them I would stay in the home of the youth leader on Friday night (talking about the importance of being a listener and minister to him and his family), have breakfast on Saturday with the family, and go with them to their youth outing. Saturday night I planned to stay in the home of the pastor, spending time with him, listening to his problems (so many pastors are very lonely because they cannot share their troubles with their congregation). After breakfast with his family on Sunday morning, we would go to church, and I would speak in a Sunday school class (I love small groups) as well as in the service. Sunday afternoon, the plan was to meet with some of the members of the missions committee for lunch along with the pastor and his wife. The plan for Sunday evening was a short drive to another church in a nearby town to preach and then stay in the home of the pastor or youth leader.

Trying to stretch dollars, I would stay in the area through Monday and Tuesday, going to a pastors' fellowship, meeting with a new pastor who had moved to the area to serve in another church, and making phone calls to organize our next major activity for young people (Basketball Marathon, Super Bowl, etc.). I taught how to save money by doing as much ministry as possible before traveling back home. Keep in mind that cell phones had not been invented, so long-distance charges would eat up a budget very quickly. Therefore, making local phone calls from a home in that area saved money.

Next to those dates, I wrote estimated amounts for fuel and meals. I moved to Wednesday through Saturday of that week to show my plan for office work, preparing mailings to promote the large events or a prayer letter, phone calls that I needed to make, and so on. I wrote down costs for printing and postage for office work. I circled my day off and a special family outing that we planned for Saturday when the kids would be off from school. This was not for ministry expenses, but I wanted to show how to plan a calendar that would include time for family as well as ministry.

After completing the plan for the entire month, we ran a total for expenses for that month. I could see the lights starting to come on as the men approached the task of preparing a budget with new vigor. One of them exclaimed, "Now this is starting to make sense. All right!"

Each man worked on a plan for six months. Occasionally, I was called to come to look at one man's plan or answer a couple of questions. We stopped to evaluate our work for the first six month of the next year. Two of the men let out a groan after realizing that they had a deficit because more money would be spent than what would be coming in. This led to a discussion about the need to raise more support. So we reworked the income line, making goals about how much new support needed to be raised. One man finally admitted that he had to make some cuts because he had not been realistic enough in the past. We looked at each other with renewed respect. We were in this together as a team. Again, the lights were coming on as the men were realizing the big picture.

After reworking the first six months, we attacked the next six months with more enthusiasm. As a result, we came out with a balanced budget with realistic goals for both income and expenses. One of the men was asked to "present and defend" his plan for ministry for the next year. He did an excellent job. He was all smiles at the conclusion as he looked at the rest of the team and said, "Man, this is starting to make sense. For the first time, I feel like I've got a handle on my ministry finances as well as my personal finances. Hey, I put some notes on my calendar as to what we will spend or save as a family. This really helped."

Helped me too! Thank you, Lord, for this idea! This idea will help you with your ministry plan for this year as well as next year. Use it to plan out your personal family budget using a calendar. It may help you do more ministry for the Lord with fiscal soundness as well as manage your personal finances.

Memories That Haunt

You lie down for a nap—zap! Or, you are just about to go to sleep at night—zap! Or, someone says something that triggers an old memory—zap! An old haunting memory comes to your mind. How do you handle this?

You are not alone, as most of us have to deal with this. As you might surmise, these thoughts come from the wicked one, Old Scratch, the devil, Satan. It's a battle for all of us. Paul refers to this in 2 Corinthians 10:5, "Casting down imaginations, and every high thing that exalteth itself against the knowledge of God, and bringing into captivity every thought to the obedience of Christ." So I think we are safe to say that the apostle Paul struggled with this as well. Satan has access to our minds and is very clever, knowing when to jab us with an old haunting memory.

Memories such as the time you were mistreated or rejected. Or when a close friend turned on you, much to your surprise and chagrin. Perhaps it was an experience when you lost it in a fit of rage, saying something that you deeply regret. The examples are numerous for all of us.

First thing to do—ask God to forgive us of all bad experiences when we wronged someone or forgive those who wronged us. Jesus touched on this in the Lord's Prayer. But those memories come back to our minds when we are relaxed or unguarded. I usually turn my attention to the Lord, saying, "Uh oh, Satan is attacking me again, Lord. Help me with this. I've already asked you to forgive me, and I assure you that I've forgiven the other person. But here is the devil again haunting me with this old memory. I give this to you right now because I can't handle this. I need your help now." Then I force my mind to think about something nice, something special (Philippians 4:8–9). For example, I start thanking the Lord for my wife or for how He helped me today or for the beautiful sunset—you name it. I kick myself into the thankfulness gear. Helps me so, so much.

In a nutshell, deal with the past. Forgive. There is no other quick-fix solution. Give it to God. Why? A clean slate, a clean heart gives Satan less to take advantage of. Then become proactive with thankfulness. This changes the mind, the heart, the soul. It's like telling yourself, "I'm involving God in this by thanking Him. I'm turning a negative into a positive." This quickly changes the mood, the environment in your heart and mind.

I suppose I should warn you that if you dwell on the old negative memory, getting yourself worked up feeling anger, resentment, frustration, and so on, you need to ask God to forgive you of the new emotions, the new sin. I know we are all human and it takes a few seconds to realize what is going on in our minds. Learn to do this as quickly as possible. Otherwise, you will be headed for a downward spiral, a nosedive to destruction.

Call upon God for His help as quickly as possible. Over time, we can learn to do this even more quickly. God will help us. I assure you that He is helping me.

More Is Caught Than What Is Taught

No one discipled me after I came to Christ. I've listened to others say the same thing, as they lamented not having anyone to teach them what to do as a new believer. Please do not misunderstand, as I am all for discipleship. My experience has been that more is caught than what is taught.

In other words, open your eyes and pay close attention. Watch your leaders. Do the same as they do. Be careful, because you will see human failure. The same is true for those who are watching you.

It was a privilege for me to be mentored directly by Jack Wyrtzen, the founder of Word of Life. He would tell stories to drive home points he wanted to make. For example, I noticed that he told me the same story on three different occasions. It seemed he really wanted me to learn what he was telling me. When he started his story on the third occasion, I told him that he had already told me this and that I had implemented it into my life. "Really? Did you finally get it?" His voice boomed, "Ha!" as he slapped my leg. "You finally got it. I wondered if I would ever get through to you. Ha! Tell me how you have been using this in your life." After sharing a couple of examples, his voice softened. "You got it, buddy. You got it. Don't ever stop doing this." What was he trying to teach me? *Accept people for who they are and see them for what they can become.* That philosophy is how I am wired today. He taught me to see potential in people without condemning them because of where they were at in their lives at the present time.

Harry Bollback mentored me as well with a completely different approach. Whenever I would ask Harry a question about ministry or the Christian life, he would say something like, "Oh golly, Eric, I don't know. I just do it. I mean, well, you know, uh, I just do it. It's just what you're supposed to do." Guess what? That did not discourage me. I learned tons of stuff from Harry as I chased his coattails, following him around. I mean to tell you, this man can really get things done and has accomplished so much, touching tens of thousands of lives. No, hundreds of thousands of lives. With Harry, I learned that more is caught than what is taught. I had to keep my eyes open and watch. "If it's worth doing, it's worth doing right!" was one of the many wise statements coming from him. "Dream big, then exceed those dreams" was another one. "It doesn't matter what people think of you; it only matters what Almighty God knows about you," was one of his favorite phrases when speaking to teenagers.

Two great leaders with completely different styles, both impacting my life in a tremendous way. I am thankful to God for these men. One of my special memories from traveling with these men in evangelistic meetings was listening to some of their phone conversations. Jack was slightly more than ten years older than Harry. When I was with Jack, he would tell me that he needed to call Harry. You would never have known that there was ten years' difference in their ages. Jack's face would light up when he was able to get Harry on the phone. "Hey, buddy, how's it going?" His love for Harry was evident in his voice as well as in the expression of Jack's face. Later, I would be with Harry when he called Jack on the phone—it was so similar—Harry's face was aglow, beaming as he exclaimed, "Hey, boss. Oh my, God is abundantly blessing here. It's amazing!" What a privilege for me to have witnessed this on numerous occasions.

Yes, I was watching, and I caught it. I got it!

Another great leader in Word of Life spent quality time discipling me—Mike Calhoun. I noticed Mike pulling out some white cards with something printed on them, which made me curious. In a nonchalant way, he told me that he was working on some scripture memory verses. Boy, he suckered me in with this casual approach. I was hooked. I was hungry for more and more, full of questions. Mike taught me to spend quality time building up a man and that the ministry would grow. "Build the man first, Eric, and God will build the ministry." He would phrase it a half of dozen different ways over the years, but it had the same principle. That is, invest in a person, teaching him or her how to feed him or herself spiritually, and the ministry will be an outgrowth from the person's spiritual growth. Very biblical approach.

Truth is, every man that I have mentioned in this article used a biblical approach. The disciples were watching Jesus all the time. Sometimes they listened to Him as He taught. At times they watched His actions. What is the old adage? "Actions speak louder than words."

Two takeaways for you: (1) Watch your leaders and learn; (2) invest your time, energy, and prayers in the young leaders under your care.

My Boss Is My Friend

My boss is my friend, yet he is my boss. How do I balance this relationship?

I had a boss who was also my mentor—and he was my dear friend. To this day, he remains a special friend. When we first connected, we had an immediate friendship. We really clicked. He was two years younger than me, but this did not make a difference. It felt like he was five years ahead of me, spiritually speaking. He was growing in the Lord, and I wanted what he had. Therefore, we had a great friendship.

After two years, he became my boss, and I found this to be a great relationship as well. I strived to make him successful, and he did the same for me. There were special moments in our friendship that were more friend-to-friend than boss-to-employee. Yet I could sense when it was time to move back to the employee-boss relationship. Imagine your hands extended in front of you, side by side. Turn your hands so that fingers face fingers, horizontal, level. This symbolizes the friend-to-friend relationship. When it is time to return to the boss-to-employee relationship, move one hand under the other, with the upper hand symbolizing your boss. Sometimes the friendship can be on a horizontal basis, whereas most of the time it is on a vertical basis—that is, you report to a boss.

Just for a moment imagine what it might feel like if you were the boss having a great friendship with someone who works for you. You, as the boss, need friendship, and you enjoy hanging out with the staff member. What if this staff member had such a high level of respect and honor for you as the boss? So high and so respectful that you could relax enough to really enjoy the special friendship that is so good for both of you. And this staff member would be so alert that he would sense when it was time to get back to work, and he would report to you as the boss. Do you think this would be an incredible blessing for both of you? This is what my boss and I had. And you can have it as well. Put yourself in the shoes of your boss. That is, think about it from his or her side, his or her perspective, not just your side. This will help you see things in a much better way. It just might help you to honor your boss with respect and enjoy the incredible friendship that will only grow stronger.

There are certain topics that come up during these moments of fellowship where your boss may feel that he or she needs to gently encourage you or teach you. Please do not be hurt, because he or she is mentoring you with great love. Your gentle response, accepting these words, will strengthen the relationship. It might feel like you have just been moved back to the worker role, but this is not the case. There will be certain themes talked about that your authority realizes he or she needs to say something to help you grow. Becoming offended and hurt hinders the sweetness of your fellowship. If so, your boss has to move back to the boss-employee position. It will take much time to get back to the sweet fellowship you enjoyed earlier.

As the friendship grows between the two of you, there will be some moments when your boss will be vulnerable, sharing some of his or her difficulties. It is a great honor for you to be trusted enough that your boss will open up to you. You may be shocked at what he or she tells you. Or surprised. Don't be. We all struggle, and this includes me at times. The apostle Paul speaks of bearing one another's burdens as mentioned in Galatians 6:2. We must do this because we are told to do this. We need each other. Do not look down on him or her. Most importantly, keep your lips zipped. Do not tell others. Instead, take it to the Lord in silent prayer. Meanwhile, when your boss opens up to you, look for an opportunity to affirm him or her, to encourage him or her. Your boss needs this just as much as you do. Later in the conversation, they will apologize for talking about their struggles. Assure them you care and you are thankful they could be transparent. Let them know that this has actually helped you because it is good for you to see how they handle the bumps in the road that life brings. Over the next week or two, your boss may be looking at you to see if you disrespect him or her, or that you are disappointed. Give a warm smile, letting your boss know the friendship is strong and it is a privilege to serve on his or her team. This will do wonders for your boss and for you.

Consider Proverbs 22:11 (ESV), "He who loves purity of heart, and whose speech is gracious, will have the king as his friend." Whenever you read the word "king" in Proverbs, think of your leader, your boss. No, he or she is not a king or queen, but kings were the leaders back in those days. Notice the two things that will strengthen your relationship—purity of heart and gracious, kind words as you communicate with your boss. There is no place for disrespectful words to your boss or behind his or her back. Is this how you want your friends to treat you?

In review, honor and respect are vital keys in building a friendship with your boss. Don't be afraid to ask them what you can do to help them. Look for ways to be a blessing. Does your boss have a favorite type of coffee? A favorite sandwich or dessert? Dig into your pocket and buy it as a special treat every so often. Is there a book your boss has been talking about wanting to read? When you are on a trip, be ready to jump out at a pit stop to wash the windshield as well as get rid of the trash in the car. Little things like this means so much. Let them know that you are praying for them and let them know you are always here for them if they need a listening ear. One more thing—when your boss tells you something that is private or a secret—never ever tell anyone else.

After a year or two, you will have a wonderful, deep friendship, which will mean so much to you and to your boss. Enjoy!

Ol' Ben Franklin Had a Good Idea

Years ago I read Benjamin Franklin's autobiography. At age twenty, he was determined to excel in thirteen virtues to improve his life. It piqued my interest because I sensed there were some things I needed to change in my life, such as becoming kinder to everyone.

Mr. Franklin worked on the following virtues, seeking to improve himself: temperance, silence, order, resolution, frugality, industry (work ethic), sincerity, justice, moderation, cleanliness, tranquility, chastity, and humility. You do not have to use the same character traits. You could use eight items or whatever number you choose.

The old inventor worked on each character trait one week at a time. He made notes to serve as reminders, placing them around his home and office where he would see them. Making a conscious effort every day to improve his life, he found that this had a profound impact. At the end of thirteen weeks, he made a new list, keeping some of them because he felt he still needed to work on them. He deleted the areas where he believed he had made significant improvement, and he added some new traits that he wanted to acquire or improve. Over the course of three or four years, he had made great strides becoming a better gentleman, which was quite important during the time in which he lived. In fact, this focus improved every area of his life, as he realized he was much more disciplined than ever before. He continued to rise in prominence to the extent of being an ambassador for the young United States to the nation of France. He helped with the founding of the United States and assisted with the writing of the Constitution. He was an inventor and a great entrepreneur.

Eventually, Mr. Franklin arrived at his core virtues, the thirteen as mentioned. He printed evaluation forms to check his progress as well as daily to-do lists, implementing his core virtues into his daily plan.

It is not certain if the writer of *Poor Richard's Almanac* was a believer or not. He was considered to be a Deist, and he meditated upon God and the Bible. In fact, he wrote a commentary on the Bible that was more of an intellectual book of observations about the scriptures.

Still, his idea is worthy of consideration, and I used this for a period of time. It would be of value for me to use this again in my life. I can tell you that some of these disciplines helped me very much at a critical time in my life in my thirties as I greatly benefited from this practice. And others benefited because of my efforts and discipline.

To bring things into a Christian perspective, I used Bible verses to solidify my desire to grow and to improve. Ephesians 4:32 has stayed with me to the present day, as I focus on becoming kinder to everyone.

One Proverb Daily—Gaining Wisdom from God

Way back, years ago, I started reading a proverb a day. On the first day of the month, I read chapter 1, and on the second day chapter 2, continuing this to the end of the month. The next month, I started over reading through the book of Proverbs, one chapter a day. Yes, I still do this.

Amazing wisdom can be gleaned from Proverbs. Many of the verses give you a good example and bad example. You can choose which example to follow. You can recoil from the bad example to quickly choose the good example. This is great for teenagers as well as for adults.

It's good for men and women to read. Let's admit it, sometimes we get stuck in a rut, a bad habit. Any person, at any time, can start in Proverbs to garner wisdom on a daily basis. It's worth the effort. I cannot recommend it highly enough.

I'm convinced that we can learn the mind of God by reading Proverbs and memorizing scripture. Both inject God's Word into our minds and hearts. It is revolutionary, life changing.

One of the best moves you can make in your life is to read a proverb a day. Don't wait until the first of the month. Start today, now. For example, if today is the fifteenth of the month, read chapter 15. So much practical wisdom will be right at your fingertips. Later, it will be in your mind, influencing your thinking in a very positive way.

Highlight important verses with a marker or use a pen to underline. You may want to use a notebook and use one page for each topic or theme, such as leadership, self-control, pride or scoffers or fear. Write out the entire verse in your notebook under the appropriate heading that you create. Review it later when faced with a problem or worry. Hey, why not memorize these verses? This will become an invaluable resource for you.

Enjoy! Start today, please.

Opportunities To Partner

There are many missions in the world doing an outstanding job. Most of these works have a targeted focus, such as church planting, student work on college campuses, youth camps, leadership development, Bible institutes, and much more. Generally speaking, each of them had a special beginning with an outstanding founder. Each developed an identity that makes them unique.

Over the years, some of these organizations join together because of leadership needs, financial difficulties, or almost identical philosophies of ministry. This happens after the third or fourth generation of leadership, after the founder has passed away. I have seen this happen with church denominations joining together as well as mission organizations uniting.

Every now and then, there are partnerships for a special occasion—Summer or Winter Olympics, a large event that attracts attention across an entire continent, a world-renown evangelist or singer bringing together tens of thousands of people. There are attempts to bring together groups of a lesser nature. There are various reasons for this, which need to be carefully considered before becoming involved.

Usually one partner will be stronger than the other one. Will this actually help your mission or are you contributing time, resources, and manpower to help the larger group? More importantly, will the partnership cause your mission to lose its focus? Do you really know what your focus is? If so, I urge you to take time and pray before getting yourself involved in a partnership in ministry.

Yes, I have had experience working with another organization in a partnership. There were personal friends working for the other group. I knew them well, and I knew the founder of the other group quite well. We wanted to help our nation with church planting even though this was not our main focus in ministry. We tried to meet a need. We could place some of our graduates as pastors in the new church plants, and they would send their young people to our youth camps. Excellent aims and goals. The other group needed some fresh blood, manpower—our graduates from our Bible institute. There were some wonderful things accomplished in this partnership. Occasionally, we looked at each other wondering why there were some misunderstandings. But we were able to work out each of these issues. Actually, the word "issues" is too strong. They were not serious problems at all. We continued the partnership for about five years, thanking God for what was accomplished.

There was another opportunity that I refused because I knew there would be compromise in doctrine. Over the years, I turned down all other requests. Why? I knew that each one would get us off of our main focus. It is important to keep the main thing, the main thing. Otherwise, it becomes a focus on the minor instead of concentrating on the major.

Spending large amounts of time hammering out the details of a partnership leads me to conclude that I have already taken my attention away from our main focus. In other words, I look at most partnership ideas as an opportunity to say no. If you are a dynamic leader, you look very appealing to other groups. They may want to use you to enhance what they are doing. Is this the right thing to do? My opinion is to keep my focus on what God has called me to do rather than get sidetracked.

Please, I am not trying to be harsh or rude. Keep the main thing—the main thing.

People Follow What You Are For, Not What You Are Against

Being raised in an era when pastors and religious leaders were known more for what they were against, I have learned that people follow what I am for, not what I'm against.

Don't get me wrong. I know that there are sins named in the Bible. God is not for things that are evil. And I know that we live in a day and time when people do not like the word sin. This is not what I am talking about.

Personally, I believe in a positive approach that shows people what I am for. People love a positive emphasis, enthusiasm, and commitment. As we continue to move forward, I am able to teach what the Bible says regarding good and evil. I do so in a positive way, meaning that I do not condemn others. Those who follow my life will see what I am for and notice what I do not do.

People will never see me drink alcohol. It simply will not happen. However, I do not crusade against this. Many Christians do not have a problem drinking alcohol. It wasn't always this way, but this is the situation today. My lifestyle shows a different choice, but I do not criticize those whose choices differ from mine.

If you enter my sphere of influence, you will see and hear what I am for, not what I am against. As a result, you will be energized to follow a positive influence.

I remember a time when religious leaders were known by what camp (group) they were in and what camp(s) or group(s) they were against. If you were not in their camp, you were ostracized and rudely condemned. I know because I weathered many a storm like this and survived quite well. I stood my ground with a confident smile. Still smiling—with confidence.

One day the disciples of John the Baptist came running to their master, telling him that Jesus was baptizing more people than John. John humbly responded that He must increase and I must decrease (John 3:26–30).

Mark 9:40 gives another example; as the disciples saw someone casting out demons in Jesus's name, they told him to stop doing this. But Jesus told them not to say that to the man because if he was not against them, then he was for them. Luke 11:23 says it this way: "He that is not with me is against me, and he that gathereth not with me scattereth."

It is my conclusion that emphasizing the negative, what you are against, scatters rather than attracts.

Planning

Someone said, "If you fail to plan, you plan to fail." Well said.

Proverbs 16:1–3, 9, 25, 33 says, "To humans belong the plans of the heart, but from the Lord comes the proper answer of the tongue. 2 All a person's ways seem pure to them, but motives are weighed by the Lord. 3 Commit to the Lord whatever you do, and he will establish your plans. 9 In their hearts humans plan their course, but the Lord establishes their steps. 25 There is a way that appears to be right, but in the end it leads to death. 33 The lot is cast into the lap, but its every decision is from the Lord" (NIV).

Luke 14:28 says, "For which of you, desiring to build a tower, does not first sit down and count the cost, whether he has enough to complete it?" (ESV).

With four five-year plans and two ten-year plans under my belt, with about forty years of experience as a missionary leader, I know the value of planning. Oh yes, during three years as a pastor and three more as a youth pastor, I worked on some one-year plans and three-year plans in my early twenties before serving as a missionary. It took a few years of experience to make a plan beyond one year. As I recall, I survived from week to week during my first year in the ministry. There was no mentor available, so I started reading materials written by Ted Engstrom and Edward Dayton, among others. I discovered that I needed a plan.

A wise pastor asked me what I thought I would be doing in my ministry in the next three years. Then he moved to five years after I gave some vague answers at age twenty-four. I was overwhelmed when he asked about my plan for the next ten years. But these questions prompted me to think and make a plan. Becoming a voracious reader, not only Christian books but also books on business and leadership, helped me to be able to talk with business people. Picking their brains, I learned many things to help me prepare a five-year plan. As I said, I worked on four sets of five-year plans before embarking on my first ten-year plan. These tiny steps, by faith, got me going in planning.

It was gratifying to accomplish many of the goals in these plans. Some were not fulfilled, only to be reevaluated or added to the next plan. As a young pastor, I searched the Bible for something I had heard in a message or lecture when I was a university student. Long before the days of Google, I searched and searched until I found Luke 14:28. I was a twenty-three-year-old pastor trying to "lead" a church to relocate from one area of Atlanta out to the suburbs in North Atlanta. We were negotiating a loan from the bank for the purchase of an old, historic church building. Some of the members wanted to relocate, whereas 25 percent of them refused to budge. I thank God for some wonderful Christian businessmen in our church who helped with all of this. We prayerfully sought the Lord according to the maxim found in Luke 14:28.

Along the way, I found that the Bible had more things to say about planning. Proverbs 16 is a masterpiece. It covers anything from a daily plan to a monthly plan, a yearly plan—five years, ten years—you name it. From this chapter I learned to cooperate with the Lord in making a plan. First, I would "dream on paper," writing down my thoughts. Then I would pray asking the Lord to lead, guide, and direct. I trusted Proverbs 16:1–3, especially the third verse, "Commit to the Lord whatever you do, and he will establish your plans" (NIV). I would take the rough draft and go to verse 9, asking the Lord to establish my steps. Verse 25 is a warning that, at first, there is a way that seems right, but the end is death. I prayed again, asking God to check my motives, as I only wanted His will, not mine. As I navigated through the first few months of the plan, I learned to make adjustments as I watched the sovereignty of God unfold. In other words, some things did not go as planned, but God changed them according to His master plan. I learned to be thankful for this, even though there were a few times I was scratching my head, trying to figure things out. But the less I did of that, the more I learned to be happy as God directed my steps.

Ask yourself this question: "What do I want my ministry to look like by this time next year? In three years?" Take a deep breath and ask yourself about five years and ten years. Can you visualize these changes or growth? What steps do you need to take to get there, to realize these goals? Did you think about your personal growth—spiritual, mental, and physical? You are part of the plan, so you should plan your growth in these areas. You will literally grow with the ministry. If you don't grow, neither will the ministry. Make a list of goals. Write down potential problems that you foresee. What might hinder you from reaching these goals? Write this down so you will think about them, taking them to God in prayer, asking for His help. Finances needed? How will you fund your goals, your plan? Did you put down specific dates to accomplish certain goals? Be realistic. I had some friends, leaders, who wrote down unrealistic goals. Each year when we would meet, there would be a report of how many came to Christ as compared to our goals set last year. I would watch these men hang their heads as they came way below what they had planned. Then I listened as they set even higher goals for the next year. It was a vicious cycle that I wanted no part of. I set realistic goals enough to stretch me and rejoiced when I exceeded these goals, praising God.

Accountability: You have this working as a member of a team. During your weekly or monthly meetings, there may be a time to check on goals to see how the master plan is working. You can motivate each other to do your best for Christ. It is very healthy to do this. If you are working alone, you need someone with whom you can share your plan. Get back together for follow-up to give an account. This will also help you make some modifications in your plan because you may not see everything working alone. Proverbs teaches the value of good counsel.

Work your plan every day. Break down the overall plan into quarterly, then monthly, then weekly goals. Set dates. Push yourself to meet these self-imposed deadlines. Use this whether your task is a program director, discipler, cook, maintenance staff, event promoter—every position on the team is part of the overall plan. If you are struggling to get out the promotion (flyers, e-mails, text messages, phone calls), you have not been working your plan. If you fail, pick yourself up and try again. Consider this as a learning experience. What did you learn? How will you improve? Write it down and include specific dates to get the job done. Don't just leave it hiding under a stack of papers. Get it out the next day and add tasks to whatever daily to-do list you are using. This keeps it in front of you. If you do not have a daily to-do list—start one today. You're now on your way to learning the fine art of planning.

Powerless without God

I can't do anything without God.

You already know this—that you are powerless without God. Let me ask you, do you acknowledge this in everything you do? Everything? Even the routine tasks that you can do with your eyes closed? I mean *everything*. To be honest, I'm still learning this. One thing that I know as I age—I am powerless without God.

God has gifted me with several talents, and I am grateful. You are gifted as well. Some have more talents and abilities than others. My father taught me years ago that there will always be someone smarter than me or who has more ability than I have. It was very good advice for me. I do not envy those who have more abilities than I have. Daddy helped me to see this. Nor do I look down on those who have less abilities or talents. I feel that I am balanced in this. But talented and gifted people usually rely on their abilities to get them by, to accomplish their goals. Less on God, more on how good they are. Be very careful here. Very careful. God is watching, and He knows our innermost thoughts, even if we do not say them.

With great emphasis, I encourage you to admit that you are powerless without God. I am powerless, despite my talents. Why not yield myself to the Lord, asking Him to empower me and profusely praise Him afterwards? How about you? One telltale way of knowing that people know they are powerless without God is that you will hear them give glory to God, praising the Lord, after they finish a project or after they finish speaking to a group or singing a solo or a group song. Doesn't matter what the project is—uploading a new web page, printing a new camp brochure, a successful phone call with a new convert, cleaning the floor—you name it— anything and everything.

You and I are powerless without God. Lavish Him with praise. "Thank You, Lord, for helping me get this job done. I realize without Your great power, I can do nothing. I praise You and thank You." God *loves* to hear this. After all He has done for us, giving us His only Son, Jesus Christ, He deserves our praise. Don't you feel good, refreshed, blessed after you thank and praise the Lord? Just for a second, you feel very humble as you say this to God. Then your spirit soars. I call this a win-win. It's good for God, and it's good for you. How incredible and awesome God is to give you a boost, a blessing *after* you praise Him. Wow! My heart is in orbit just writing this for you. What a privilege to be able to praise and thank God!

Pride: Road to Failure

God must really hate pride because the scriptures are full of verses and examples regarding this subject. It is at the root of all sin, along with rebellion, as Lucifer, the angel who rebelled against God, was full of pride (Isa. 14:12–14).

Nearly every person struggles with this in life. So what is the antidote? Humility.

Whereas God detests a proud heart, He loves a humble heart. In fact, before honor and promotion comes humility. If you have a haughty, proud heart, God is against you.

So, what do we do to move from pride to humility?

Evaluate what you have been saying. Go back and think about some strong statements that you've made in the past. Do you often tell others what *you* have done or do you give God the credit? Ask your wife or husband if she or he thinks you struggle with pride. Don't be mad if the answer is yes. By the way, if you did get mad when you asked your mate or a close friend, it means that you are prideful.

Scratching your head trying to figure out what to do? First, humbly ask God to forgive you of this sin. Second, search the scriptures on the topic of pride, noting how much God despises pride. Write them down and memorize some of them, referring to this list often. Third, develop a fear of the Lord, a reverential respect, because the Word tells us that the fear of the Lord is to hate pride. Fourth, give God the credit for everything you do. I mean everything. In doing so, it brings you to the fifth point, which is change your self-talk and your thinking patterns. The old nature for you was to tell yourself, "I can do this," or, "If it's to be, it's up to me." Instead, use Philippians 4:13, "I can do all things through—Christ—which gives me strength." Truth is you and I can't do *anything* without God's help. Zero, nada, nothing at all without God's help. So, acknowledge this in your prayers and in your self-talk, along with monitoring/changing what you are saying to others. You will come to notice pride in others as you look around. Show them mercy—that's how you used to be, maybe worse.

Funny experience, I once fell on the stage on the way to the pulpit. As I got up, I quipped, "Looks like I have a problem with pride because the Bible says that pride comes before a fall." The audience was laughing. Later, one young man told me that what I said and how I reacted really ministered to him, teaching him. We had a short talk about the truth of that statement as he admitted that he struggled with pride.

Am I past this sin? Do I have still have pride? Sorry to say, that old beast, pride, hangs around, and I have to do the five things that I suggested to you. In fact, I asked a famous pastor, who was in his late eighties at the time, if he ever struggled with pride. "It's still a battle, son. You never completely get past this because Satan is a roaring lion seeking whom he can devour. This is one of the things that men will trip up on, until the grave. Just don't let them 'trip' you into the grave," he chuckled. Wise, very wise statement.

Here are some positive examples for you to use:

"We had an incredible meeting with many saved. My, God blessed, giving me strength. Thank you, Lord."

"Tough experience last week—I could not have made it through without the Lord's help. God is good. He's good all the time."

Someone once gushed to me, "Oh, Eric, you are so talented. You can do it all. Lead a meeting, sing, be funny, be serious, preach, and the front is full of young people coming to Christ. What is there that you can't do?"

"God did it! I am nothing without Him. God gets the glory!"

The lady came right back with, "But God used you, so you can take credit for that."

"Dear friend, the emphasis is on God. I am totally powerless without Him. I am so thankful for His help and power," I said, shaking my head side and side.

She just wouldn't give up, coming back with "You're too humble. You were great."

To which I pointed to heaven, smiling, saying, "God gets the glory," ending the conversation. (True experience.)

Yes, it's a battle. Fight it with statements to praise God and give glory to Him. He is watching very carefully—very carefully. The Lord loves your praise and your humble heart.

Recruiting Camp Counselors

I
t never ends. If you are involved in a youth camp ministry, you will always be recruiting camp counselors.

Going through the cobwebs of my brain, I remember the months before our youth camp in Hungary opened in 1990. The country had just broken away from Communism in the fall of 1989. It was a different world there at that time—so different from modern-day Hungary.

One of the first things I did when I moved to Budapest was to ask pastors and church leaders if I could come to their churches to speak and promote the youth camp. The vast majority were very open to me as an American with a translator coming to their churches. There was a great harvest as I did evangelism in their churches. After all, they had not been allowed to give public invitations for people to receive Christ during the forty-five-year period that they called the Difficult Years.

So I preached in the church services, as well as giving an explanation of what the new youth camp experience would be like. Each time, I gave the dates of our counselor training sessions, asking for young adults eighteen and older to join us. After the meetings, I would talk with some of them as they inquired about more details.

See the chapter "Tell Why" for details regarding their responses during the first training sessions.

Shortly after the end of the first youth camp season, I started the process all over again— recruiting more camp counselors. We were adding three more weeks the next summer, bringing us up to ten weeks of summer camp. I knew we would need a minimum of twenty-five to thirty counselors each week. After two years, I began to realize that this process would never end, as I would always be recruiting camp counselors.

The reason for this is that most young adults in their college years had three or four summers they could offer to us. Many of the campers loved their counselors so much that they wanted to become camp counselors when they became old enough. Then it helped when we started a Bible institute, in that one of the requirements was for them to earn credit by serving as camp counselors. Still, I had to recruit counselors from churches because the number of counselors increased to about thirty-five each week as the number of campers increased.

This recruitment helped build the relationship with the churches, which is critical for a youth camp. It was a great joy for me to see some of our experienced camp counselors take leading roles in their churches when they became older. Can you imagine my joy when the camp counselors from our first years had married and brought their children to our camp? They would bring their children to me, "Uncle" Eric, recounting the wonderful experiences they had when they came to camp when they were younger. Their children would look at me with deep respect. It was so special. By now, some of their grandchildren are coming to the same camp.

It was worth the effort to spend the time every year traveling to all of those churches, preaching the Gospel and recruiting camp counselors.

Relationships with Churches

P arachurch organizations need to build strong relationships with churches, which can be a blessing for churches. For more than thirty-eight years I have forged deep, loving partnerships with churches.

First, pastors are lonely. It's a tough, demanding life for a pastor. They feel that they cannot confide in their church members, so they feel somewhat estranged and all alone. At times, denominational leaders can help, but they are busy and have plenty of challenges of their own. If you are serving with a parachurch organization, you have a unique opportunity to minister to pastors and their families.

Ask for an appointment to meet with the pastor to become acquainted. Take a quick look around his office to see where his interests lie. A family picture, his diploma, sports team memorabilia, special photos, etc. To help get the conversation going, comment on one or two photos, asking to see his family or something about an interesting photo on his wall. Who doesn't enjoy talking about their family? It will show that you care about him.

After asking about his church and how things are going, take a few minutes to talk about your ministry. But don't go on and on. Some positive, upbeat statements about a recent youth camp or evangelistic outreach will be of interest to him. Then move the conversation back to him. "Pastor, our ministry cannot exist without strong relationships with churches and with pastors such as you. We want to be a blessing to your church, not a hindrance, not a threat. We are not here to build an empire. We are here to reach young people for Christ, and we need solid churches to send these young people to. And you need a trustworthy place to send the youth of your church. To me, it seems that we can partner together, and I hope you will agree. Quite honestly, right now I just want to build a friendship with you. To care about you and find out how I can help you, encourage you and pray for you. I am being as upfront and open as I possibly can be by saying these things. So, my dear brother, please tell me how you are *really* doing. How can I pray for you?"

Saying these things will open the door to begin to build a long lasting friendship with a dear man of God. He needs you. And you need him. We are in this ministry together. No one is an island. We need each other. I can tell you from experience that I have some wonderful friendships with some godly pastors, which have gone on for years and years. I have stayed up late at night, listening to them pour their hearts out. Yes, I ask to stay in their homes when I return for a visit. You can accomplish so, so much by staying in their homes, eating some meals together (dinner and breakfast the next morning). You meet their wives and their children. Learn their names—write them in a notebook to refer to when you pray for them. These pastors will begin to open up to you, sharing deep, personal prayer requests regarding one of their children who is struggling or difficult issues in their churches that perplex them as to what to do. Pray together aloud. Oh, dear friend, these pastors *need* you so much. Take these words to heart and you will have an incredible ministry—behind the scenes—that will help both you and the pastors in your public ministry.

Remember what Paul said to Barnabas a few months after their first missionary journey. "And some days after Paul said unto Barnabas, Let us go again and visit our brethren in every city where we have preached the word of the Lord, and see how they do" (Acts 15:36). Then, they left Jerusalem to start their second missionary journey. Herein is a biblical foundation for a ministry with pastors and their churches. Go visit them often. Some will become favorite places for you to go, so make certain that you don't go to the same pastors again and again. Be sure to visit other pastors as well. After a few years, you will see how God is using you with a very unique ministry, a very fruitful one at that.

Kindly ask to preach in their churches and to the youth groups. Some churches have small groups, which is something that I enjoy. It is easier to build relationships with small groups. I always want to speak in the church services, yet I look for opportunities to speak with small groups because there are parents of the young people in these groups. Parents need to get to know you.

As the churches begin to trust you by sending their young people to the youth camps, you will not only see some of them receive Christ, but you will also see some of them desire to become camp counselors. By the way, it is a great joy after ten to fifteen years to see the children of the original camp counselors come to youth camp. Later, some of them will become camp counselors just like their parents did twenty years earlier. Who knows? You may be able to see the grandchildren of some of your counselors become campers, and then they become camp counselors. What a blessing!

You may have to convince certain pastors that you are not "stealing" their young people. Show them how your ministry is reaching them for Christ, discipling them and helping to build up the church. Most churches cannot develop youth camps or conduct evangelistic outreach programs for a large group of youth from a wide, geographic area. Admit that there may be one or two young people who will want to join your mission someday, but this will be something that their church can take great pride in. The vast majority of their youth will "come back" to their churches. Point out the fact that many young adults in their twenties move away from their home country to seek employment in another country. But they return to visit, bringing money to help their families. It is simply a fact that churches have to deal with in this present-day world economy. So, in a way, their youth are "stolen" because they cannot find good jobs to provide a good salary. Some pastors have not thought about it this way.

Regarding pastors who live in the city where you live, it probably would not work out to spend a night in their homes. However, you can meet for coffee after your initial visit at their churches.

It takes time to build trust. Treat pastors like you want to be treated. Love them, spend time with them, pray for them and with them. Truly care about the struggles that they are going through. Send a text, e-mail, or a handwritten note through the mail to let them know you are praying and that you care. This is greatly appreciated. I know this from experience because I am still doing this very thing with a number of pastors that I know.

Resisting Authority—Bad Move

Ever have someone under your care resist your authority? Have you asked yourself why some people respond this way?

It's a defensive mechanism system they have because of something that happened in their past that was painful. It may have happened because this worker's father abandoned the family or they watched their parents' divorce or they were deeply hurt by another leader.

I watched this with one man who grew up very poor because his father left the family. He was the oldest child, protective and proactive over his siblings. He had become the man of the family, trying to make up for his father. It was a defense system that he carried over into the ministry. He was resistant, not teachable, proud, and arrogant. Yet he had tremendous potential.

How do you convince such a person that the old system is not needed now? God is his authority, yet God uses leadership in our lives. God sets up the authority of leadership over us, and we are to respond well in both small and big situations. Seek to please authority and you please God as a result. Well, it's not an easy task.

Nothing will happen until he chooses a new belief system. More than this, he has to trust God. He suffered pain in the past, and whether he realizes it or not, he does not trust God now. No progress can be made until he breaks down the barriers that he has erected, repents of his actions, and trusts the authority that God has placed over him.

I mentioned how my mentor Mike Calhoun believes in the principle of "Build the man first, then build the ministry." I accepted this philosophy and will always do this in raising up new leaders. To get a person from point A to point B, you have to win their trust, using the principle of servant leadership. Win their heart and you will be able to disciple them.

Perhaps the "Nathan method" would work best. The prophet Nathan approached King David, describing something that happened that was not right. The king was incensed that what this unknown person had done was very wrong and must be punished. Then Nathan looked directly into David's eyes, telling him that he was the man who had done this. As you know, Nathan was revealing that God knew the sin David had with Bathsheba and what had happened to Bathsheba's husband. The idea here was to get David to see his sin from another viewpoint so he could be led to admit his sin and confess it to God. David did confess to God with a contrite heart in deep sorrow for his sin. See Psalm 51.

Before you do this, be sure to look deep into your heart regarding your personal response to authority. If there is a problem, deal with it. Then you can move forward just as the prophet Nathan did.

May God give you wisdom because if you take apart a person, you have to know how to put them back together again. Kindly ask the younger person if they are willing and ready to change their attitude and thinking. Be gentle but firm. If there is resistance, tell the Nathan story and show how David quickly changed, confessing to God. Then ask the one in your care if they will do the same.

They may do as you kindly ask or they may resist. If you err, err on the side of grace to give them one more chance. Yes, this is one more chance than the prophet Nathan gave. Tell them that you will meet with them again, one more time. As you set a time to meet again, tell them that you love them and pray for them. Let them know that at the next meeting you will be expecting a genuine, spiritual change or you may have to make a change. As you can see, this is used only in a very serious situation.

At the next meeting, have a Bible study with your young colleague, teaching what God says about authority in Romans 13:1–2 and 1 Peter 2:13–25. Ask if they understand this point, or at that point help lead them to a favorable response.

Explain that the Bible teaches that children are to be submissive to their parents (Eph. 6:1–3). Plus, wives to their husbands (Eph. 5:22; 1 Pet. 3:1). Church members to their pastors (Heb. 13:17; 1 Cor. 16:15–16). Employees to their employers (Eph. 6:5; Col. 3:22; 1 Pet. 2:13–14) and all believers to each other (Eph. 5:21; 1 Pet. 5:5). Lastly, all believers to God (James 4:7; Rom. 6:13).

Giving the person a second chance gives time for the Holy Spirit to minister to them, giving them time to think and pray. It gives you time to make certain that you are calm and in control of your emotions. Plus, it creates a positive form of pressure with a deadline and a final decision.

Even if they do not respond favorably when you meet again, letting them go might be the best spiritual medicine they will ever receive. It just might be the best thing for them.

Respect for authority is a serious matter, as God takes this very seriously.

Revenge Is God's Business—Not Ours

"Dearly beloved, avenge not yourselves, but rather give place unto wrath: for it is written, Vengeance is mine, I will repay, saith the Lord" (Rom. 12:19). Christian ministry is not impervious to deals that go bad or to being cheated. Just as business dealings are sometimes crooked in the corporate world, the same can be true for believers. The temptation is to get even, to gain revenge. No, no, no! Don't do it! Let God handle it. He will do a far better job than you or I will. I've seen this again and again.

Satan will bring it to your mind in subtle ways. It will gnaw at you, and you will seethe within.

So, what do we do? Forgive!

Say what? Come again? Yes, forgive them. In fact, if you ever have opportunity to do so, do something nice for those who hurt you. Romans 12:20 takes a cue from the book of Proverbs, "Therefore if thine enemy hunger, feed him; if he thirst, give him drink: for in so doing thou shalt heap coals of fire on his head." Proverbs 25:22 concludes with "and the Lord shall reward thee." How about that? Turn the other cheek and do good to the one who conned you or tricked you. In doing so, you will totally confuse them with your goodness and kindness. This is counter to what the world does; however, this approach allows God to work in their lives because of your gentle and merciful response.

However, if you take revenge, trying to get even, you allow bitterness and anger to develop. The end result is not good at all. Who is the one who is hurt twice over? You! You were hurt when you were lied to, and you will be hurt if you take revenge. Furthermore, God will not move forward with His perfect vengeance. Instead, the Lord will deal with you because of your anger and immaturity.

This is graduate-level Christianity. Not easy to do, but God will help you. Let God handle the matter, and He will do so within His perfect time schedule. You may never know the final result. But you will grow in the Lord, becoming more Christ-like. Jesus Christ did not take vengeance on those who lied about Him, betrayed Him, or crucified Him. He is the perfect example in how to handle the temptation of revenge.

Zip your lip and take the situation to God. Pour your heart out to Him, and He will listen. When I have a difficult situation, I pray to God, raising my open hands palms up and putting the problem into my hands. As I lift up my hands in the air, I pray, "God, I can't handle this. I give it to You. Now, it's Your problem, not mine. I turn it over completely to You." This is a great help for me, as it takes a ton of pressure off of my shoulders.

When the devil puts evil thoughts into my mind, I immediately take this to the Lord again. "Lord, I gave You this problem already. The evil one is trying to upset me. I will not take revenge. Again, I need Your help, and I trust You with all of my heart to take care of this." You may have to do this more than once, becoming stronger each time if you do as I suggest. This has really helped me. And God is pleased.

Wait! Warning! Don't rejoice or laugh at the one who mistreated you when God takes His vengeance upon him, or God will immediately stop (Prov. 24:17–18). The point here is that God is at work as He deals with the other person. If you or I say, "Ha! Serves him right," God will stop the punishment and turn His attention toward you or me, to correct our wrong response. God does not want us to think we are better than others or to become haughty. The right response to God's vengeance is to pray for the one who wronged you, to show pity, mercy, and kindness.

"Blessed are ye, when men shall revile you, and persecute you, and shall say all manner of evil against you falsely, for my sake" (Matthew 5:11).

Seeing Potential

Gideon was minding his own business, doing his regular job despite the difficult times that he lived in. The Midianites were in control, causing God's people much suffering. You may recall the story of an angel appearing before Gideon and calling out to him, "Oh, mighty warrior!" *Who me?* I wondered about Gideon's thoughts as he looked at the angel with the deer-in-the-headlights stare. *Surely the angel has to be talking about somebody else.*

God needed Gideon to step up to be the leader to help His people, knowing that Mr. Unknown has vast potential. God sees us for what we will become, not for who we are right now. The Almighty wants us to grow, to realize our potential. The same is true for you and me.

One area where God has gifted me is seeing potential in people. My eyes are always scanning the crowd looking for individuals with potential. We need future leaders, and they need to be recognized and developed.

For example, in 2001, a young Romanian student enrolled in our Bible institute in Hungary. I noticed him on the first day, snapping my fingers, saying aloud, "*This* young man has tons of potential!" One of my top staff members overheard my statement and started focusing on the young guy. Later in the year at a banquet, Iulian Avramescu came to my table to serve me my favorite drink at that time, Pepsi Maxx. Smiling, I said, "You're the future!" I had no idea at that time that we would be working together six years later. In fact, he is directing our work in Romania today, doing an outstanding job.

Look for leadership qualities, teachability, a combination of boldness and humility, a growing love for God. There are more qualities, but this is a good start. Then spend time with that person to take them to the next level. I call it getting him from point A to point B, then to point C and so forth.

Keep your eyes open for certain potential leaders who can take secondary roles. Not everyone can play the role of the second person, the assistant director, the Joshua position. This is how to build a team, that is, looking for young leaders who can minister in different roles on a team. You look for loyalty, team spirit, dedication, a work ethic, a penchant for excellence.

Yes, there have been some flameouts along the way. But I've seen some superstar leaders developed as well. In fact, I have several stories I would love to tell you regarding these superstars. I am blessed as I watch them from afar or up close. Love it!

Keep your eyes peeled—be on the lookout for potential leaders—there are mighty warriors out there. Pray that God will lead you to them.

Sensitivity

Some people struggle with sensitivity. This is true with some leaders as well as staff members. It is wise to know what is behind this behavior. It is only a symptom, so it is best to try to identify and correct the cause rather than treat the symptom.

The root cause is insecurity. Many young people struggle with this because of abuse or some traumatic experience during their childhood such as separation, divorce, or death of a parent. This leads us to ask, what is the source of their insecurity, which leads us to something deeper—fear.

Let's go back to the issue of sensitivity. Does the person have an attitude that everything is just about him or her? This is a faulty perception because each of us is a part of a larger community such as family, classmates, colleagues at work, a church, or a staff.

There may be a more difficult situation if you, as the leader, struggle with sensitivity because you are more isolated with less intervention. You are going to have to take this to the Lord and yield this to Him, asking for help. Those who are totally honest with themselves can make progress with this issue. Most people don't want to give up the layers of protection that they have formed to spare themselves from pain. Are you one of the ones who want freedom from this negative problem? If so, answer the following questions.

—Have I frustrated others who told me that I'm too sensitive? Have more than one or two people told you this?

—Do I enjoy my personal frustration when I'm sensitive and insecure? Probably, you do not enjoy this at all, if you were to be completely honest with yourself.

—Am I willing to ask God to help me with this problem?

—Am I willing to forgive those who caused me suffering and pain? Can I forgive someone who has betrayed me?

—Am I ready to do this—right now?

—Did you do this?

—Can you trust God now? Completely?

Let me assure you that negative feelings or thoughts will rise to the surface in the future. If you truly forgave the one(s) who hurt you in the past, you do not need to ask for forgiveness again. That's a done deal. When God forgives, He completely forgives, and He forgets about it. You and I may not be able to forget about it, but God promises that He does. So when the ugly thoughts come up again, ask God for His help for these present thoughts, reminding Him that you asked for His forgiveness and you know that He forgave you. Tell Him that Satan is causing you trouble with these old memories. Then simply ask His forgiveness for these present thoughts. This may be repeated several times, so do the same thing each time. You grow in your relationship with the Lord as the old things of the past lose their strong grip on you. I can tell you that I know this from personal experience—it works.

Do a study in the Bible on "trust." Commit some of these verses to memory and you will grow exponentially. You will be thrilled with the new you. More than this, you will be thrilled in your awe of God that He meets your needs.

God will test you by presenting situations or people in your life that will put you in a vulnerable position of trusting others. Jacob was a very fearful man, particularly when he had to face his estranged brother, Esau. God tested Jacob, and his relationship with God grew deeper as God protected his life from his enraged brother. But I must admit that you might be let down again at some point in your life in the future. Not by God. By others. Take it as a test and go through the steps I have mentioned already, yielding it to God. Pass this test and you will enter into a much deeper relationship with God.

When people struggle with sensitivity, they have blinded themselves from seeing the bigger picture. Weaving a cocoon of protection, every effort is made to protect from future pain. The focus is on self rather than what God is doing. Joseph was sold into slavery by his dysfunctional, jealous brothers. His father, Jacob, thought he was dead. Joseph went through more suffering in Egypt when he was thrust into a prison for thirteen years, having done nothing wrong. It was a terrible injustice. Yet, Joseph came out of this experience at age thirty without bitterness or anger. It is one of the most amazing stories in the Bible. Later, he met his dear father and forgave his brothers. My point is that it may take years to see and understand that God is in control and that He is working behind the scenes on your behalf. Trust Him for the bigger picture that you cannot see right now from your viewpoint. He may reveal His bigger plan for your life in time. You can trust God—always.

Set the Pace

Christ set the pace for us by living a life without sin. Blows my mind. and I'm sure that this is hard for you to fathom as well. But He did it! Absolutely no sin even though He faced temptations just like you and me. He set the pace with His obedience throughout His life all the way to the cross. In death, He was obedient to God the Father. Yes, He set the pace.

Men and women admire pacesetters. Young people do as well. Many people love to be challenged to do their best. They love a positive example—setting the pace. Quoting Dr. Lee Roberson, "Everything rises or falls on leadership." (6)

Christ did it when He arose early to pray. Yes, He was the Son of God, but He was a man and He realized that He needed to connect with God the Father. So, Jesus set the pace in prayer by arising early to have private prayer. This is one example of many that Jesus was a pacesetter.

Set the pace in prayer. Then lead the way in Bible reading, reading good Christian books, in witnessing, in giving, in service, and more. Why? People look up to a pacesetter. Pacesetters set the standard. We all need an example.

Think about the pacesetters that have influenced you and your ministry. Write down what you learned from them. Actually, this is how I started a series of articles on leadership. I wrote down what I learned from each great man who influenced my life, my growth, and development in Christ. Then I wrote what I did for my team members (giving God the glory).

Next, make a commitment to be a pacesetter for your staff, your team. Circle the special things that your pacesetters did for you and do the same for those within your sphere of influence. Possibly, there will be one or two more areas where you will feel you should set the pace for your team.

Are you frustrated with some of them? You can influence them by being a pacesetter. Go the extra mile, being a servant to them. This will catch their attention because people love to be served. Yes, it will take time for this to be noticed. I've found that more leadership principles are caught than taught. Tell your team the things that you've noticed in the lives of your mentors, your pacesetters. Share stories of how you observed their lives and how this influenced you. Train your staff to become people watchers, especially those in leadership. Of course, they will be watching you. Don't mess it up by announcing to them that you are their pacesetter. Just teach them to be observant of leaders who are presently influencing their lives. They will watch you with more interest and will slowly be influenced by you setting the pace.

After all, this is exactly what Jesus did. Enough said.

Setting the Example

What a special time. Jack Wyrtzen, my hero, my mentor, asked me to walk with him. We were on Word of Life Island near Schroon Lake, New York, during the summer of 1979. I was new to Jack's ministry although I had heard him speak at a university ten years earlier when I was nineteen. I was captivated by every word Jack spoke whether it was from the pulpit or when taking a walk together.

After a few steps, Jack bent over to pick up some litter on the path. He was telling a wonderful story, and I was soaking in every word. About twenty paces later, he bent over again, picking up an ice-cream wrapper someone had dropped. A minute later, he repeated this action. By now I was scanning the path looking for little pieces of paper, rushing a couple steps ahead to pick up a gum wrapper.

Without saying a word about what he was doing, Jack was setting an example for me. I commented on this, and he said that if everyone would pitch in and help, we could have a clean youth camp. I got it! I got the message.

To this day I do the same, as my eyes scour the sidewalks and beyond looking for items that young people have discarded without thinking. In fact, years ago I convinced our camp program director in Hungary that one of the activities I wanted him to organize was to have two teams competing to see which one could pick up the most trash. As I told him about this, I bent over to pick up some paper on the sidewalk. A few steps later, he rushed ahead to get the next candy wrapper.

He got it.

Success (Christlikeness) Starts with a Choice

Success is a buzzword in leadership books. It's a hot word because everybody wants to be successful. Please allow me to suggest that instead of using "success," let's use "Christlikeness." For a follower of Christ, success is being Christ-like, that is, becoming more like Christ.

Additional hot buzzwords out there are "Five Easy, Fast Steps to Success." The author wants you to think that if you do what he or she suggests, it will be easy. And fast. Just five easy, fast steps and voila—success. Friend, becoming more like Christ takes a lifetime. It's a slow process, and generally speaking, it's not easy.

Now that I've popped your balloon, let's get started. Becoming like Christ starts with a choice. The very first choice is to receive Him into your heart and life. In case you have never made this decision, go to the back of the book for an explanation of how to receive Christ.

After this, the big choice is to dedicate yourself to the daily task of becoming more like Christ. Have you done this? I would suggest that you pray this prayer right now if you have never done this. "Dear God, I am willing to do whatever You would have me to do in my life, my family, my work, in everything. I give myself completely to You, dedicating my life to You."

There are many choices after this. Decide to read the Bible through in one year. You will need to read five chapters a day. It will be a thrilling odyssey for you. In addition to this, read one chapter from the book of Proverbs daily. There are thirty-one chapters in Proverbs, so read the first chapter on the first day of the month and continue. Underline verses that really stick out to you in Proverbs. Why? You will gain much wisdom reading Proverbs month after month. No, not just one month. Read it again the next month and the month after that and so forth. Continue to do this for years and years. It will literally fill your mind with wisdom. You will better understand what God's will is for your life and how to handle personal problems. After two or three years, your mind will immediately think of a verse in Proverbs to help you handle a special situation that has arisen in your life. It's amazing what this will do for you.

Not finished. More choices to make. Memorize scripture, the great verses. You can Google this topic to come up with extensive lists of verses to memorize. Take the time and effort to do this. Want to know why to do this? Well, if there is one thing that you can do to speed up the process of becoming more Christ-like, it is memorizing scripture. It literally changes how you think. You are memorizing the Word, the holy scripture. It is powerful like a double-edged sword. It's like putting the Word of God into your mind. At least, it's a good start at doing this. Do you have a major sin that dogs you, paralyzes you? Memorize verses on that subject. This will help you so much to clean up areas of weakness. There's nothing quite like it. Do it!

No, we're not done yet. Prayer is next, although it's not necessarily in this order. We need to pray the first day that we receive Christ. And the day after. Skip back to my chapter called "Change the World through Prayer" after you finish this one. Set a definite time and place to pray. I can't say this strong enough. You have to make a serious choice here. I'm not talking about a morning person or a night owl, using this as an excuse. Choose an exact time when you will pray and a definite spot, a certain chair in a certain room or a certain place where you will get on your knees. Otherwise, you will be inconsistent. Through consistent, regular prayer we can change the world. You need a notebook or create a prayer list on your iPad, iPhone, or laptop. Here are some headings to choose: My family, my friends, my neighbors, my work. Or, my ministry, my missionaries, my pastor, my supporters, my plans and goals, my unsaved list, my staff or workers, nations of the world—the list goes on and on. Guard your special time. The results will be incredible! You will soon be putting a check sign or "prayer answered" on request after request. It will build your faith like nothing else.

Faithful church attendance at a sound Bible-preaching church is very important. Meeting with an accountability partner is vital (see "Accountability, Good or Bad Idea?"). Choose to tithe. Oh, did I mention reading a good Christian book or two each month? Later you can add new topics or things to do as you grow in Christ.

Lots of choices to make. The ball is in your court—make your next choice.

Look at my chapter called "Growth Is Not an Option" where I describe how to make a spiritual growth chart. If I feel a lull in my spiritual life, I will pull out a fresh copy of this chart, writing down what I want to work on daily and checking off each day when I have completed my Bible reading, prayer list, or whatever.

Take the Next Step

Moses led the nation of Israel out of their bondage and slavery in Egypt, following instructions from God not to take the normal trade route. They ended up at a dead end with the Red Sea before them on one side, enormous mountains to the south and to the west. Coming from the north was Pharaoh and his army, having decided to give chase to put God's people back into slavery. In human eyes, there was no escape.

God's people were crying out to Moses in fear and anguish, wishing they had never left Egypt. Moses prayed to God for help. As far as I know, this is the only time in the Bible that God told a man to stop praying. What God the Father did say was for Moses to take the next step.

It was the biggest step in his life—into the Red Sea. God wanted to show the nations of Egypt and Israel, as well as all of the nations on earth, how great and powerful He is. An incredible miracle was performed with the parting of the waters when Moses took the next step. Not only did God move back the water to create a way to walk across the Red Sea, He also made the ground dry. Moses led a group of about two million people on dry ground, which was about one mile wide. It was one of the most incredible miracles in the Bible.

God created a heavy fog so that Pharaoh's forces had trouble finding their way while Moses led the people across. The Almighty lifted the fog when His people were safely on the other side, allowing the enemy army to use the same path through the Red Sea until all of the soldiers and chariots were on their way across. Then God allowed the water to close together again, drowning all of the Egyptians. God showed His mighty power in a great, demonstrative way.

None of this would have happened had Moses not taken the next step.

There will be a time in your ministry or in your work when you will have to take the next step. If you do not take that step of faith, you will slide several steps backward or fail.

It may be the decision to dedicate your life to the Lord, being willing to serve Him. Or it may be a major decision to get advanced training. For an experienced leader, it may be the moment that you purchase land or a building to expand your ministry or business. In fact, there may be more than one "next step" moments in your life.

Such a decision sets the course for the rest of your life, shaping your destiny. Claim Joshua 1:9 and take the next step—God will be with you.

Tell Why

W hen I started our youth camp in Hungary, the country had just become free
after being a Communist nation for forty-five years. People were very quiet,
whispering in conversations in restaurants. During the Difficult Years, as
the Hungarians called the time under Communism, people were very careful not to talk
too loudly, lest some Communist party member might overhear a conversation and then
report back to the leaders. The result could be disastrous for them.

So when we held our first camp counselor training in March 1990 in Budapest, the
young adults present were so, so quiet. After all, the Russian soldiers were still occupying
Hungary even though they were a free nation. The Hungarians were afraid that the
Russians would never leave. Were they really a free people yet?

It seemed like I was talking to a wall when I was teaching a seminar on the philosophy
of youth camps. I was explaining how we would run our first youth camp, scheduled to
open in the summer of 1990. It seemed as though I just couldn't get through to them, or
that's what my impression was. Later, I learned they were listening very carefully.

At the conclusion of that first counselor training with nineteen present, I asked how
many of them wanted to be a camp counselor that summer. I was crushed when not
one of them raised their hands to volunteer. Not one of them. Thinking quickly, while
sending up a quick prayer, I smiled, announcing our next camp counselor training in
April. Encouraging them to come, I asked them to bring one of their friends who might be
interested in this. I told them that I was new in the country and I didn't know many people
yet. No one nodded, signifying yes. Nada. Zip. Nothing. (Swallow, breath deep, smile.)

In the meantime, I spoke in as many Hungarian churches as I could each Sunday,
which was a minimum of two churches and sometimes as many as four churches.

The churches would schedule their meetings at various times throughout the day to accommodate my schedule. They enjoyed having a speaker from the United States and were keenly interested in the new youth camp at the famous Andrassy Castle in the small town of Toalmas, Hungary.

Soon it was time for our second counselor training, and I started with some hidden fear and trepidation. I knew at the end I would ask for volunteers, and I wondered if they would sign up. Oh boy. Whew! During that meeting, I was describing some games we would play with the campers (crowd breakers, etc.). In the spur of the moment, I asked them to show me a Hungarian game, and they quickly responded.

We made a big circle with two of them chosen to be blindfolded. One would call out "here," and the other would muffle his voice saying "there." They couldn't see each other as they were trying to find each other in this big circle. They would try to "throw" their voices, trying to trick the other person while reaching, searching for the other one. It was fun to watch. A couple of times "here" would bump into the circle, and the other counselors would spin him around back into the open area of the circle. Same thing happened to "there." Finally, one caught the other, pulling off his blindfold, and everyone cheered. They played the game a couple of times until a guy said, "Eric, you put the blindfold on and get into the middle." Oh my, here we go. I agreed, putting on the blindfold. One of the Hungarian guys was putting on a blindfold as well. I was calling out "here," and this guy was saying "there." I seemed to not be making any progress at all until it dawned on me—nobody is "there." I stopped to laugh and slap my legs with my hands, and then I pulled the blindfold off. Nobody was there in the middle. That boy had slipped off his blindfold and joined the circle. They got me! I laughed and laughed.

That broke the ice. See, I didn't get upset or angry because I had been "made a fool of." I laughed, and they loved me for it. Everyone joined in for a big laugh. It was the most noise I had heard since my first trip to Budapest in July 1989. It was great!

Thirty-two young adults were on hand for the second training. So that part was going well. We were growing in number. The response to my teaching was much better, probably because they saw that I could laugh at myself and not be offended by their pranks. When I got to the end, with much anxiety on the inside yet with a big smile on the outside, I asked how many would like to be a camp counselor. Would you believe that not one of them raised their hands? Well, believe it because that's what happened.

Looking at their somber faces, I said, "Okay, we will have only one more training session in the month of May. We open the camp in June. At the next counselor training, I will ask you at the end how many want to be a camp counselor. I really have to know if you will do this or not. And I need to know which week or weeks you will be a camp counselor. Why? Because I told you earlier that we will only take a certain number of campers based upon our number of counselors. We want to have a quality ratio of six or seven campers to one counselor. Why? Because if we have ten or twelve campers and only one counselor, it is too many. Counseling will not be as effective. We want the camp counselor to talk to the campers more than once during the week to give quality time. This is our philosophy, and we're sticking to it no matter what."

That's it! The *why question* was answered in their minds. God gave me this thought, and I used it. I did not know it at the time, but this was the catalyst that engendered their response at the final training session.

We had fifty-eight young adults at the last one. Wow! I was pumped. I was scared too, just a bit. Okay, a whole lot. At the end, praying to God in my heart with the most enthusiasm I could muster, I asked them one more time. Reminding them what I said at the last session about why I needed to know, I pointed to a chart where they could sign up for certain weeks or for the whole summer of seven weeks of camp. Needless to say, I was sweating bullets, as one of my friends used to say.

Ladies and gentlemen, all fifty-eight of them signed up! I was happy beyond measure. We had an incredible first summer with 168 young Hungarians praying to receive Jesus Christ. Thank you, Lord!

Tell your people why. I can tell you that Europeans are like this all across the continent, not just Hungarians. Actually, all human beings are like this because they need to know why you want them to do something. It's not a battle of the will; rather, it's engaging the intellect, the brain. Explain why! This is true with staff members, especially new members to the team.

Ten Most Wanted List

Taking a cue from the FBI's Ten Most Wanted List, I wrote down a list of ten people who I wanted to become a Christian. I was just sixteen years old when I did this, having received Christ only months before at age fifteen.

My list was at the forefront in my thoughts and in my prayers. I took action on this list speaking to all ten of them and asking them to trust Christ as their Savior. Would you believe that seven out of ten made this decision? And I was at the baptism of the eighth one when I was sixty-two. It took a long time for him to make his decision.

After seeing seven out of ten becoming believers, I made a new list, adding seven more people. Within a couple of years, more joined me in the faith.

It's time for me to make another list! Here's why—we have to keep our focus on reaching people for Jesus Christ. It has to be a priority or nothing will get done. For those of us who are professional speakers, we sometimes think that preaching and teaching is enough. True, the presentation of God's Word will be blessed as Isaiah 55:11 promises. Yet you and I need to be intentional in reaching out to others.

I will never forget the anxiety and frustration I had being stuck in traffic, trying to get to the airport to pick up one of my special mentors. Twenty-five minutes late with my stomach tied up in knots, I saw him sitting on his suitcase outside the airport. My heart sank to lower depths than ever before. Oh me!

When I jumped out of the car, I was apologizing profusely when Jack Wyrtzen called out to me, "Hey, Eric, meet your new brother in Christ!" I shook the man's hand in disbelief. I was both happy for him, and I was greatly relieved. Jack had used the time to lead a young businessman to Christ! Yes, that stuck with me.

No, I do not know if Jack ever used a Ten Most Wanted List, but he was always talking to people about the Lord. It was always on Jack's mind as he reached out to people.

Whatever idea or method you use, whether it be the Ten Most Wanted List or a commitment to speak to someone every day about the Lord, just do it. Meanwhile, I will put together my next list. It will be exciting to see how many of these ten people accept Christ.

Test Time: Make an A+

The book of James speaks of temptations, trials, and tribulations: "My brethren, count it all joy when ye fall into divers temptations; Knowing this, that the trying of your faith worketh patience" (Jas. 1:2–3).

God tested His people again and again in the Old Testament, as the book of Hebrews 11:17a records for us: "By faith Abraham, when he was tried, offered up Isaac."

Again and again in the scriptures, God tried the hearts of his servants as well as the nation of Israel to see what was in their hearts. Ultimately, He knows what we will do when confronted with a choice that stymies us or that tempts us. He wants to see how we will respond. He tests us to help us grow.

Jesus forewarned us that we will have tribulation in this world. John 16:33 says, "These things I have spoken unto you, that in me ye might have peace. In the world ye shall have tribulation: but be of good cheer; I have overcome the world." Therefore, we should not be surprised when we have difficult experiences. Embrace difficulty, trials, and tests. Rather than trying to get out from under the tough time, accept it with trust in God. Realize that God is using this to shape you and mold you into what He wants you to become.

Think about how your mentors handled tests in their lives. Do you recall one of them telling you a story how he struggled with a tough situation until he realized that God was using it to bring about change in his life?

Let's talk about the subject of brokenness. Joseph, in Genesis, is a prime example of a broken man. What is unique about his story is that he had done nothing wrong. Jealous brothers sold him into slavery. Talk about a dysfunctional family! Thrown into prison when he chose purity instead of caving into the advances of Potiphar's wife. Not fair, right? Once in prison, someone he helped promised to put in a good word to help him get out of prison. The man lied, forgetting his promise to Joseph. Why did God do this? Joseph was in the prime of his life from age seventeen to thirty. His youth was wasted, so it seemed. Not so! God knew that He needed a broken man who would not be arrogant and revengeful when He put him into power to save God's people. Eventually, Jacob's sons came to Egypt to purchase grain, and Joseph could have crushed them by throwing them into the worst prison in the land. But he did not. He showed them compassion, grace, and mercy. In doing so, a humble and wise Joseph spared the nation of Israel from starvation and death.

Moses was broken after he killed an Egyptian, living in the desert for forty years while raising his family. He was a changed man who God used to free His people from slavery in Egypt. There are numerous examples throughout the Bible.

God broke me as well. One notable experience was the death of my right-hand man in Hungary, Dan Bubar. I agonized over his road accident while he languished in a coma. Less than two weeks later, he went to be with the Lord at age twenty-nine. What did I do while he was in the coma? I was at his side in the hospital until his parents could arrive three days later. I pressed into God, totally devastated. I had to go to the roots of my salvation, putting my complete trust in God. Later, I reviewed my life since that life-changing experience. I was left with the overwhelming thought that God is good, even if I don't understand what has happened. The book of Psalms resounds with verses that proclaim that God is good. David knew this well and loved to tell all who would listen to him.

Building on a foundation that God is good, using Romans 8:28, I noted that whatever God brings into our life is for our good. Have you noticed that the word "bad" is not in this verse? We define things that happen as "good" or "bad." Could it be that God defines all of them as good? Well, they are for our good, so this must be true. We look at life from our own perspective, whereas God looks at you and me from His divine perspective, as to what is best for us.

God is good and even if I don't understand what is happening to me or why it is happening—I trust Him. From there I choose to press into God, receiving this for my good, choosing to be obedient, taking the next step to follow Him. How about you?

Yes, my faith was tried again in the death of my wife, Lynne, in December 2013. As early as 2007, I could see this coming because of her disease, multiple sclerosis. She had the type of MS that never improves. Sensing that God would take her home at some point, I leaned on God with faith and trust. During her physical decline and horrific pain in her suffering, I never ceased to say that God is good. This helped me through the biggest test in my life so far. I say this only to praise God rather than to heap praise upon myself.

God is good all the time!

Thankfulness, the Key to Growing Close to God

A thankful spirit gives room for God to work in your life. God loves to hear the praise of a grateful believer. In 1 Thessalonians 5:18, it says, "In every thing give thanks: for this is the will of God in Christ Jesus concerning you."

What is the secret to becoming more thankful? When we express it several times a day to God or to others, we become even more thankful. It's making a decision to give thanks—for everything. You are literally programming your mind and your heart to be more thankful.

Again and again in the scriptures, we are told to "Give thanks to the Lord, for He is good." Check out Psalms 107:1, 136:1, as well as chapters 118 and 136. In 1 Chronicles 16:34, it says the same thing.

The more you trust God, the more you are able to receive His blessings. One of the best ways that I know to open myself up to God is to thank Him. For what? Everything and I mean everything. Even the difficult things that come into your life. In fact, thanking God for the tough times has a way of helping you through it. As a result, you trust more. This really, really works.

On the opposite end of the spectrum is an unthankful spirit. This person complains all the time—negative, resentful. He or she becomes jealous of those who are happy, sneering at those who are thankful. I know enough about Proverbs to move away from that person or I will become like them. I am too happy to allow someone with an ungrateful spirit to pull me down because I want to stay happy, to remain thankful.

If you have a staff member or colleague who is struggling with this, I encourage you to reach out to this person in love. Speak kindly, showing sincere interest in encouraging them. Try to lovingly bring them to repentance because they are spiritually sick, on a downward spiral. Do not allow yourself to be dragged down to their level. In fact, this is exactly what they will try to do, to level you, to bring you down. They know they are not happy, or they are insecure, resenting your happy, thankful spirit. They think if they make you become ungrateful and unhappy, they will feel better. This is a lie from Satan. It will only make things worse for them as well as you. It is a spiritual problem—sin. If you cannot kindly bring them to repentance, have nothing to do with them, even if it means removing them from your staff. They will only poison the rest of the team.

Meanwhile, you can grow in your thankfulness every day. Paul said this is God's will. It must have been very important or Paul would not have written this to us. The Holy Spirit inspired him what to write, so we know that God considers thankfulness to be very important. Chase it with all of your heart.

Tell God how thankful you are for your salvation, the Word of God, His promises, His creation. Thank Him for the water you drink, the food you eat, for the one who prepared the food or gave it to you. Thank God for your wife or husband, girlfriend or boyfriend, for your children. Thank Him for your parents. Thank Him for the difficult neighbor who lives next door, for the difficult boss that you have—for everything.

Read the Word, pray, memorize scripture, tell others about Christ, and much more— all with a thankful spirit and attitude. As a result, you grow in the Lord by leaps and bounds.

(By the way, I thank God for *you*!)

The Art of Delegation

You are familiar with the story about the father-in-law of Moses, Jethro, watching his son-in-law exhausting himself trying to meet the needs of everyone. The older man went to Moses in love, kindly asking him to consider getting help, delegating responsibility to qualified people. Excellent advice that Moses heeded.

Another story comes from the early church in Acts 6 when deacons were being chosen to help the spiritual leaders of the church. Great move. As your ministry grows, you will realize that you simply cannot do everything. Train young men and women to join your team, giving them things to do to help you accomplish what God has put on your heart to do.

First, pray for the right ones to join your team. You will find them attracted to your ministry in your early years. Spend time with them telling them stories of how you first started the ministry. Give credit and praise to God, as this builds a positive spirit in these future staff members. Give them things to do—little tasks, small jobs. As they hunger for more action, give them bigger tasks, lavishing much praise upon them, thanking them. Meet once a week if you can to eat together, pray together, and share your heart, your vision. Ask them to become more involved, admitting that you cannot do everything.

If at all possible, hang out with each of them individually, giving them some private time. Don't be afraid to be vulnerable, sharing what God is teaching you. If you tell one of your shortcomings, be sure to tell them what God is changing in you and how He is helping you to grow. Why? They struggle too. They need to know that you are a real person who has ups and downs. Tell how God is helping you. They will soak this up and feel close to you. Colossians 1:28 is not just about preaching and teaching. It is also about modeling a changed life as you rub shoulders working together with a staff. So much is caught by those close to you watching your life. It's not all taught. Very important lesson here.

It's time for a job description. Write down what you want them to do. Go over this by explaining both "what" and "why." You are teaching a philosophy of ministry by doing so. Most people do not move forward with the "what" until they clearly understand the "why."

Ask for an agreement that they accept the job description. Tell them that you will get together with them later to go over the job description, to see if they have any questions or if you can help them. Many leaders struggle with this, as they are busy and forget to follow up and check up. Then you are frustrated and disillusioned. You owe it to your staff member to do this. See the chapter called "You Get What You Inspect."

Some leaders struggle with letting go, allowing the team member to do his or her job. Empower this person to do his or her job. But do not do this without checking up at a later time to see how they are doing.

Get organized by keeping a file or making a chart or something that will remind you to think about your staff as to what they are doing and how they are doing it. I like to think about this when I pray for each person on my team. It is right on my prayer list I am using every day. It is in front of my eyes and on my heart—every day.

We all have our different leadership types. I once knew a micromanager who wanted to control everything. And I mean everything. This is not delegation, so be careful here. You will frustrate the person who is working for you as well as yourself. It is a fine art to let go but not let go too much. May God give you wisdom to know the difference.

Diligence and faithfulness in small tasks leads to greater responsibility. It is part of the growth process. As you see your staff member growing, give him or her bigger jobs to do. Tell them what you see and praise them. Over a few months, you will recognize their talents and skills. Get this person into what we call their "sweet spot." As a result, they will prosper and grow. Keep teaching them how to feed themselves spiritually, love them, praise them—you are going to have an incredible team member.

Think ahead to envision what you see this person doing five to ten years from now. As they mature, taking on more responsibility, tell them what you see. If he can keep their head on straight after you tell them, then disciple them each step of the way to get them there. Adjust their job description accordingly.

Truly, delegation is one of the tools God uses to build His church. It is part of the process of 2 Timothy 2:2.

The Lord Giveth and the Lord Taketh Away

My two little nieces, visiting us in Hungary, were with us at McDonald's on the outskirts of Budapest. "Uncle Eric, can I have another ice cream?"

"Sure you can, sweetheart!" And another Coke, two of them, as well as two ice creams. It was fun, and we were laughing, having a great time. We must have taken an additional thirty minutes for extra treats after eating our burgers. Time to go home.

"Oh, do we *have* to leave now? We're having so much fun."

Slowly we ambled outside to the parking lot. "Uncle Eric, where did we park?"

"Hey! Our van isn't here?"

"What happened to it?"

Three females were asking a barrage of questions while I was standing there in total silence. Finally, they looked at me, wondering if this blob of humanity would finally speak. Here's what I said:

"The Lord giveth and the Lord taketh away. Blessed be the name of the Lord."

I promise you, that's what I said. It was gone! Stolen! Vanished into the night loaded with all of our groceries, a freshly dry-cleaned Persian rug, new basketballs for basketball camp—hundreds of dollars' worth of supplies for the youth camp, and food for our guests who would come to our home for meals.

Would you believe the police refused to come to the scene of the crime? The policeman at the station growled, "Thirty-five cars are stolen each day in Budapest. You're just one of many. Come here to the station." Unbelievable! I guess I was supposed to get into my van and drive to the police station, but I just couldn't seem to find the vehicle in the parking lot where I had left it. Duh!

After calling my assistant, who also served as my main translator, she rushed to take

160

us to the police station. Suspicious why the police wouldn't come to the scene, I asked if the police were part of the crime ring that was stealing cars. Fortunately, my assistant did not translate this, protecting me. I chuckle as I think back on that.

No vehicle for the next six months, as the car insurance company was slow to pay. There was a piece of junk car that was in our fleet of cars at the mission that I could use at times. It made me appreciate what many Hungarians go through when I used public transportation. Yes, it was for my good.

I have talked about suffering loss. This will happen in your ministry or your business. What will your attitude be? How will you handle loss? Especially when you know that someone else is using what you used to have.

Job handled it as well as I have ever seen or heard of. "The Lord giveth and the Lord taketh away. Blessed be the name of the Lord." How on earth could he respond this way? Let's take a look at his response.

First, he acknowledged God, that He gives. He realized that God is sovereign and can also take away. Then Job praised God. What a saint! What a man of God! I recall reading this years ago, thinking that I would like to handle things this way should hard times come. Little did I know I would do this very thing in my life. Not only did I say this when my van was stolen, but I also repeated this statement later when my first wife died, losing her battle to disease.

What do I see in Job's statement? God, God, God. Let go of your possessions. They're not yours anyway. You're just looking after them for God, sort of a caretaker. But you say, "No, I worked for what I have." Me, me, me. That's what you're saying. Let's do it how Job taught us—God, God, God.

In case you're wondering what happened, I finally received reimbursement from the Hungarian insurance company to purchase a later model van that was even nicer than the one that was stolen. Thank you, Lord!

The Overseer Relationship

When I started a new mission in 2004, Life Impact For Eternity, I decided to operate differently than in the past, choosing to be an overseer, a mentor, rather than a strong boss telling people to do what they should do every day. There is a time and place for both leadership styles. My desire was to come alongside young men who were getting their ministries started and help them get going, to get them to the next level. So the purpose was not so much to push and demand but rather to encourage and always be there for the younger man as a resource.

Some flourish with this style, and some may not. It seems to be more like the role of a pastor who teaches, affirms, counsels, and prays. The seed is sown, and God gives the increase. Leaving the results with God, I seek to guide the young man with love. Much time is spent in prayer taking his needs to God. Not only his needs but how the young man needs to change, to grow. It is a slow process yet a healthy one. I trust God to do the unseen work to bring about change. God guides me as to what to say at the right time. Usually, before I say something, I pray, asking God for the right words and the right timing.

When can you use this style of leadership? When you are a young leader, you have to give more directives, telling workers what to do and when to get it done. You give job descriptions and you check their performance to see if they are doing what they are supposed to do. Anger or harshness slows down spiritual development in the team members. Kindness and gentleness are warmly received. Yet there are some workers who just don't get it. Judas Iscariot did not. It took a while, but Peter finally did. He was more of a bull in the china shop project. Jesus had to come down on him strongly at times. Jesus did not treat John the same way because John had a totally different personality as well as level of commitment. Thomas required time, and he always had to see it to believe it.

In the early years, you probably have to be more of a hands-on leader. You have to give direction and tell people what to do and show them how to do it. You work yourself out of jobs, replacing yourself often. After all, you were probably all alone when you first started and you had to do everything yourself. Eventually, you have a group of managers who are overseeing different sections or divisions of the ministry. How you operated in your twenties is so different from how you lead when you are in your forties and fifties. Ministering to a team of managers is more of the overseer style of leadership. And it takes time to learn how to be an overseer. You pastor your leadership team more so than you are a boss who gives direct orders like you used to do. You still do this at times but not as much as you did when you were building the mission. Grow with the changes that happen and change with the growth needs.

Dealing with staff members is a growing experience. You cannot fit everyone into the same mold, so you try to find each person's sweet spot, utilizing their gifts and abilities in the right way. This takes time, which requires patience. Sometimes you have to move one person to a different job because you learn that this is not their sweet spot. Make sure you do this in a way to build up rather than tear down.

You must continue to feed yourself spiritually. If you stop feeding yourself on a daily basis, you stunt the growth of what God called you to build up. Your prayer life deepens as you spend more time with God. You don't pray like you did in your twenties, which seemed to be more like submitting a list of needs to God. As you age, you pray for your growing leaders to become more Christ-like. You want to know more about God, and you desire to worship Him as you pray. Your list of praises is longer, and you are more thankful. What a joy to age, to mature in our relationship with God!

Your Bible study should never stop. Book studies, reading Proverbs and Psalms daily, sermon preparation—it never stops. Nor should you. Read good books and teach your staff the importance of reading along with Bible study and prayer. Someone said that what you will become in five years is what you are reading today. This includes reading the Bible.

As you grow in the Lord, and as you age, you move to the overseer relationship style of leadership. This will be a challenge for you at first because you were more hands-on in the past, more of a control type leader. Remain a control type leader and you will stunt the growth of your top managers, your top leaders. Think of it as a shepherd who watches out for the condition of their flock of sheep. They are always watching, always observant. They help the little one who is struggling or is in danger. They protect the sheep. They are always thinking about them. Do this and you will grow as an overseer, a mentor who delights in those you care for.

Timid Salesmen Have Skinny Kids

Zig Ziglar, famous motivator and salesman, is known for many great quotes, one of which is, "Timid salesmen have skinny kids." Taking a cue from the business world, he made a strong point that sales people are supposed to sell. It's what the company wants, and the sales person and their family need the salary and commissions from the sales.

Why should a missionary and their family have to suffer because they lack support? Rather than blaming potential donors, let's ask the missionary how hard he or she has worked to raise their support. Usually, the latter is the problem.

When I felt God's leading to become a missionary, I battled fear because we had adopted four children only a year or so before. Not only this, but my brother-in-law, a teenager, was living with us—five young people under our roof. All I could see in my mind was a picture of a bird bringing a worm to the nest to little baby birds, mouths open clamoring for a piece of the worm. Seven mouths to feed, including my own. Talk about pressure. Whew! Yet I felt God's call strongly, and I asked Him to provide for us. The long and the short of it is that God came through.

Yes, God came through, but He fully expected me to get out there and ask others to partner with us. It resembles making sales, doesn't it?

The Bible has a principle of asking and receiving. Ask, seek, knock. (Check out Matthew 7:7–8.) Yes, commit your needs to the Lord in prayer *and* be proactive, making a list of people and churches to pray for and to ask regarding your needs for support.

God blesses a strong work ethic. And He blesses those who call upon Him in Jesus's name in prayer. There is a fine balance here. Do both.

So, aspiring missionary, we are not talking riches here. We are talking about enough money to pay rent, utilities, clothing, and basic needs while putting food on the table. If you are single, focus on raising your full support as a single missionary. Work hard and God will bless. If you plan to be married, work on raising support for what a married couple, without children, needs for missionary support. The why should be self-explanatory. It takes time to raise new support. When you begin to date someone, you want to have time for your ministry and time to build the new relationship. May as well raise the support in advance of marriage, which makes a lot of sense. Furthermore, after you get married, you need time to build the relationship in your marriage. Having the strain of a new need of $300 to $700 per month (the amount depends upon which country you are in) to raise during the early days of your marriage can put a strain on the marriage. So, do you see my point of doing this in advance? Be wise and heed my advice. You will be happy that you did.

After marriage, you have the need to raise another $200 to $300/month to cover the needs of a baby. Have you ever checked the price of diapers? Baby food? Probably you have not done this. Expensive, to say the least.

So, back to my story with six mouths to feed as well as my gigantic mouth. I knew that I would have this vision of the little birds screaming for food at least three times a day. Pressure! I made my six-month goal in five months. I am not bragging; rather, I am sharing that I chased it because of the pressure. I made my twelve-month goal in nine months. God blessed me, and I give Him the praise. As a veteran missionary once said to me, "We have not because we ask not. So, keep asking." I simply nodded as I listened. That really helped me.

What stands in the way? Simply put, your stinking pride. Let's be honest, we all have a problem with pride. Get over it and be done with it. You are no better than anyone else, so give your pride to Jesus and go to work raising your support.

One more thing. The other problem is laziness. I've watched too many young adult Christians who somehow think that serving the Lord is like some kind of Christian welfare. Or that everyone owes you something because you have "sacrificed" and are serving God. Nobody owes you anything. Nothing. If this is your hang-up, then do us a favor by just disappearing and go back where you came from. There is no room for laziness when you serve the Lord. Potential supporters can see this, and they back away from you. Very strong, but it needs to be said.

Now, if you are still with me and you truly believe that God has called you to be a missionary, then one things remains for you to do. And that is to raise your support. Come on, let's get it done!

To Be or To Do?

In Shakespeare's *Hamlet*, the young prince, despondent as he waits for the love of his life, Ophelia, asks the question, "To be or not to be, that is the question."

"To do or not to do?" Motivational expert Michael Hyatt cleverly twisted the old bard's phrase of "To be or not to be?" to teach his clients how to get more done.

Quite frankly, earlier I chased the "to do" in my life more than I pursued the "to be." That is, I focused more on my to-do list with less attention on "to be" or what I should become in Christ. A lot of leaders have done this.

Oh yes, I had a daily quiet time, prayer, and memorized many Bible verses. One year I read fifty-two books. Another year I read the Bible through twice. There were a number of years I read it through at least once. Furthermore, I have read the book of Proverbs through each month many a month over the years. But it was somewhat hurried, somewhat rushed because I had to get going on my to-do list.

Yes, we have to work. There are goals, desires, bills to pay, and bosses to please. Yes indeed, we must work. We must achieve.

There is a fine balance in all of this. What I am finding in the final third of my life is that it is wise to focus on "to be" more than "to do." What do I mean? Becoming more like Christ, pursuing God. Could it be that I get more done by doing so? I think so.

Where are you regarding this subject? What are you doing to feed yourself spiritually? More than this, just how ardently are you pursuing God? Do you have a passion for this? What is your prayer time really like? Are you bubbling over, abounding because of your time alone with God each day?

It takes time to learn this. It is not a hasty process.

Each of us is in a certain season of life. If you are married with young children you have very limited time because of the need to care for your family—work schedule, meals, little ones being sick, the need to meet the needs of a growing family. If you have teenagers in your home, you have to give time to meet their needs. This is a different season as compared to when they were in diapers. Then the empty nest time, when all of the kids are grown and gone—a very different season of life. Later, grandchildren, which is a fun season of life. Or a messy nest when one of the children returns home to live for a period of time. These seasons of life change, and God understands this.

Still, we need to make "to be" a priority in each season of life. I am sure that you agree even though you may struggle to find an extra fifteen minutes to do so. Get up a few minutes earlier or lock yourself in your bathroom for a short time to find a place to get alone to connect with God. Have your car organized so that a Bible, a book, scripture memory cards, and/or a prayer list are available to use the time wisely when you are stuck in traffic or waiting for the red light to change. Europeans and people in other countries use public transportation, but they can still prepare for down time sitting or standing on the bus or train. All of us can get alone with God even during the hustle and bustle of moving about in daily life.

The issue here is to make it a priority to become more like Christ no matter what season of life you are in. It requires organization and preparation as well as a daily commitment.

Back to Shakespeare's line, "To be or not to be, that is the question." To do or to be?

Visualize the Future

In the summer of 1989, while visiting Communist Hungary, we visited the famous Andrassy Castle in the small village, Toalmas. We walked through the castle and around the property quickly because we had another meeting to attend in Budapest. I lingered on the soccer field as I visualized young Hungarian athletes playing soccer. Smiling, I moved on to the other side of the property where the owners had built some summer dorms. These dorms housed children who attended youth camps to listen to principles of Communism being taught.

Noting the layout of the five dorms, I decided that if we acquired this property to develop our youth camp program, a dorm in the center of the square would be our chapel. Running over there, I took a quick look inside, seeing that the dorm had four rooms. I removed these walls in my mind as I visualized a meeting room filled with Hungarian youth singing songs, laughing at a crazy skit, listening to my message, and responding to the invitation to receive Jesus Christ. My heart was stirred! I could see it well in my mind. Quickly, I decided that the back wall would have to be moved back in the center to make room for a stage where I would stand to speak. *A piano will be on the stage on this side*, I thought. *We'll have a wood background where we can hang banners. Plenty of room will be needed for dramas or choral performances.* I heard my supervisor yelling for me to hurry up, but I stopped at the entrance, deciding that we would have to knock out the wall in the center to make a sound room and have two entry doors on either side for safety precautions and easy access. Running to catch up, my boss yelled again.

Never forgetting what I had visualized, nor the sounds of laughter, the music—all of it came back to me a few months later when I moved there to begin a Christian youth camp. During that brief trip to Hungary, we were able to enter into a lease agreement to have this beautiful castle and thirteen buildings on seventy-eight acres to put smiles on young Hungarian faces.

One of the most important things that stayed in my mind was how I visualized the Hungarian youth coming forward to receive Christ as their Savior. That first summer, using the meeting room that I described, 168 young people did that very thing—asked Jesus to come into their hearts and lives.

How could I visualize this? I had been in other youth camps earlier, leading some of these camps or being the special speaker. Transferring these experiences, my mind took down walls and saw a beautiful meeting room. When the time came to do so, I worked as hard as I could to accomplish what I had visualized.

Ask God to help you visualize what your ministry will be like in the next ten years. God helped me do this, giving me the strength and resources to do so.

"Where there is no vision, the people perish" (Prov. 29:18).

Waiting upon the Lord

"They that wait upon the Lord shall renew their strength" (Isa. 40:31a).

Young people do not like to wait. Neither do young staff members. Yet God has a time schedule that is quite different from ours.

Let's look at this in reverse order. I can tell you from experience that you will know when to move forward when you have peace. Do not try to move forward on your own or you will fail miserably trying to do this in your own strength. Simply put, take the next step when you have peace. Of course, some things require provisions such as money, personnel or approval. All of these will be part of the equation for the peace that you will have from God to move ahead.

Money—sometimes you have to wait on donations to come in before you can begin a project or build a building. Then there are situations that require staff to be in place before you can move ahead, such as opening a country for ministry or a new youth camp location to run camps simultaneously. Lastly, there is the age-old hindrance of approval from a government official (zoning, health organization, bank loan, local ordinances, etc.). Wait, wait, wait.

All the while we wait, God is at work. He is teaching us patience, dependence upon Him, and building our character. Moses had to wait forty years in the wilderness for a new generation to grow up before He could lead them to the promised land. Joseph had to wait in prison from age seventeen to age thirty even though he was innocent. David had to wait in caves, hiding from King Saul who was enraged with jealousy and seeking to kill David. In fact, David had already been anointed as the next king by the prophet Samuel, but he was not allowed to assume the throne for several years. Jesus had to wait in the garden of Gethsemane, knowing that He had been betrayed and soldiers would soon come for Him. The Bible is full of examples of men and women who had to wait while God was at work. So who are you to complain? Who am I to complain?

God is really into the discipline of waiting. It is one of His favorite methods to use as He works in our lives. So, what do we do while we wait? Press into God. Why? This is what God wants us to do. As a result, God changes us—our attitude, our impatience, our arrogance, our—well, the list goes on and on. It's a matter of trust. God will let us know when it is time to move ahead. As we trust in Him, our faith grows. When we receive permission, approval, or the finances to do what we had planned, our faith explodes. Then we tell others about the "good hand of God," as Nehemiah described. God wants to show His great power at the time He knows is best for us and for all who are involved. Then He wants to receive the glory from us, praising Him and telling others how great He is.

Press into God by taking the problem to Him, telling Him you are powerless without Him and that you will not move forward until He provides for you or tells you to do so. Search the scriptures for verses to worship Him during the waiting time. Stay positive and upbeat because this is a sign that you are trusting God. He is not pleased with our griping and complaining.

Here is an example for you to consider. We were in a major building project, renovating a dormitory that could be used both for our youth camp and our Bible institute in the early 1990s. An economic downturn came about in the United States, affecting the majority of our major donors. It was like having the water pouring out of the spigot suddenly stopping with only a drip or two falling down. It was sudden and fast. The donations stopped. Zilch. Zero. Nada.

Not wanting to be in debt by taking on a bank loan, I pulled together our top leaders, telling them we would immediately halt the construction project. I explained the economic situation in the States. I told them to cover the building with plastic and tape. We stopped the project because God stopped the donations. Before I met with them, I prayed about what to tell the workers to do, giving them minor repair jobs to work on. I was cheerful and told them that God was at work and we should trust Him to provide when He was ready for us to work again on the big project. That went on for nearly a year before the funds started coming in. God tested my heart as well as my staff members. We remained joyful and hopeful while we worked on other projects that had been put off for one reason or the other. This example is not a one-time occurrence, as God has put me through this quite a few times during my thirty-eight-plus years as a missionary.

Look for things to do while you wait. Take extra time for God in your personal worship and study. Do *not* whine or complain, because God is watching. Be joyful and thank Him for the delay. Thank Him for what He is teaching you. You will experience exponential spiritual growth as you do this.

Warning: Expect a Crash after a Big Success

The great violinist gives a rousing performance with the audience on their feet clapping, begging for an encore, one more encore after another. Flowers are thrown onto the stage as people are ecstatic with their appreciation in awe of this great performer. The violinist bows to the audience, thankful for their gratitude. Finally, the musician exits the stage as the audience begins to file out, smiling one to another, raving about the performance.

It's a special night, and the soloist is on a high. Years of practice, thousands of hours of perfecting his skill led up to this rousing performance. Those in the shadows backstage are applauding the great performer as he returns their smiles. As he goes to his dressing room, he sees more flowers that fans have sent to him with notes of appreciation. He reads them one by one, and then something very strange begins to happen. He begins to critique the first solo, then the one after the intermission, and he hits his hand on the desk in frustration with himself for choosing a certain song for the encore instead of another one. Why does he do this? It was great. Fantastic! Yet he spins downward into a whirlpool of depression.

An awesome praise band, a great soprano at the opera, an eloquent speaker who gives a speech that ends with a standing ovation—there is a big letdown afterwards. It happens to realtors after they close a big multimillion-dollar sale. The wise person learns to guard against this. It could happen to a youth camp speaker, to a pastor after a great message—and the list goes on. Maybe you have already noticed this. So what do we do?

Analyzing the letdown Elijah had in 1 Kings 18, we see he was hungry and tired, drained from the great spiritual battle on Mt. Carmel against the false prophets of Baal.

He was weakened by the footrace back to town. Then he was further weakened by the trek into the wilderness when he ran away from the threats of Queen Jezebel. It was a big letdown, a crash, after a rousing success. Watch out for a crash after a big success. Be on guard for this.

Start by guarding your self-talk. Don't be hard on yourself, because you are your worst critic. Immediately give praise to God, acknowledging His great power, which gives you strength to perform or to orate. Giving praise to God is of paramount importance. Drink some water, bringing refreshment to every cell in your body. Some of those cells are in your brain. You need water ASAP. You are exhausted from your performance, so eat some protein and fresh veggies as soon as you can. You are famished. Be careful not to eat junk food or food loaded with carbs. The right kind of good food and water will replenish the reserves in your body. Keep praising God—this keeps things in perspective. So important! Get some rest, hero! You have been on a high as never before, and you cannot stay there forever. You will come down, but what I'm telling you will soften the fall, the crash. Do not allow negative thoughts to bombard your mind. This is why you keep praising God. You give Him the glory rather than do a back float in the mire of self-pity.

If you do find yourself sinking, focus on others and their needs. There is something inside of us that buoys our spirit when we reach out to others to encourage and help them. This gets the focus off of your situation. Vital. Mega important along with praising God.

Now, get out there and get ready for the next big performance. Go get 'em!

What Goes Around Comes Around

Having heard this old saying repeated to me again and again over the years, I always wondered if there is a verse in the Bible that conveys this message. Check out Proverbs 26:27, "Whoso diggeth a pit shall fall therein: and he that rolleth a stone, it will return upon him."

It boils down to how you treat people will come back to you, whether it is good or bad. If you dishonor your boss, you will find that those who report to you will not respect and honor you. They do not know that you have a problem with your authority, but somehow they pick up on it. Or could it be that God is trying to teach you something that you have never learned?

If I treat my neighbor in a nice way, I can promise you that he or she will return the good behavior. If I treat them poorly or I am rude to them, they may very well give me the same treatment, if not worse. It seems to be how life is. You get back what you put into it—good or bad.

Servant leadership is the model Jesus used. If we humble ourselves to serve the ones who work for us, rather than rule or lord over them, they will begin to do this for those who report to them. So, if we treat our managers with respect and love, they will do the same for the ones they oversee. If we are harsh to our managers, it will come back to trouble us, causing many problems. Furthermore, this behavior will be repeated throughout your organization.

This is true with your wife and children. Treat your wife with kindness, showing genuine love, and you will receive wonderful treatment in return. Harsh behavior toward her will break her heart, and she will not respect you. You will be grieved at the response. Yes, we have to discipline our children. If it is done with anger, your heart will be broken at some point because of their rebellion or because they reject you. It may not be until they leave your home after finishing their schooling. It *will* come back to haunt you.

It is so important to treat your vendors with respect and kindness. Those of us who lead ministries have to purchase goods and services. Keeping good relationships with them will come back to you in a good way. The opposite is true also.

If there is one virtue to focus on in dealing with others, it has to be kindness. Ephesians 4:32 teaches us what to do—be kind to each other.

Truly, what goes around comes around.

When a Trusted Associate Turns against You

Devastated, King David penned these words, "For it was not an enemy that reproached me; then I could have borne it: neither was it he that hated me that did magnify himself against me; then I would have hid myself from him: But it was thou, a man mine equal, my guide, and mine acquaintance" (Ps. 55:12–13).

When a trusted associated turns against you, the pain is almost unbearable. You feel as though you were sucker-punched in the solar plexus as you gasp for air. Stunned, dazed, you struggle to get through the day. At night you toss and turn. You feel as though your entire body is numb. Your heart feels dead.

Your joy has left, and you are in despair, at first. Then you are angry beyond measure. If you do not take this to God in prayer, soon you will be among the walking dead.

One of the most important lessons to learn is to take our problems to God ASAP. We are human with natural tendencies—surprised, stunned, grieved, then we rage. At what point will you go to God? Oh, dear reader, this is a battle to fight. Taking your loss, your pain, your sorrow to God as soon as you possibly can *is* the route to take.

"Why? Why? Why?" screams in your mind. God doesn't always tell us why things happen, but we must trust Him that whatever is happening in our lives is for our good. You must read the chapter "Death of a Spouse." Read Romans 8:28, applying the words to your deep pain. Yes, trust God. It has happened for a reason, even as painful as it is.

Keep in mind that God is at work (see chapter called "God Is at Work") in your former associate's life—your former partner, your coworker, your best friend, maybe your life partner. Satan comes at you with a knockout punch, a surprise attack that leaves you debilitated and wounded. Allow me to put some balm on your soul to encourage you because God is in control. This was for your good, and He will use this in the other person's life for a reason, for good. No, I can't explain all of this. After all, His ways are higher than our ways, as we find in Isaiah 55:8–9.

What's the solution? As I said, take this impossible situation to God as quickly as you can, appealing to Him for help. Next, forgive (Mt. 18:15–17). You already know how this works. If you hurt someone else, go to them asking for forgiveness. If they hurt you, forgive them. What, you can't do this? Well, the longer you languish in your pain, the longer it will hurt. The only way out is to forgive the one who was so close to you. This is the doctoral level of Christianity. If you can do this from your heart and mean it, you will grow in your faith as never before.

The strained relationship may never be the same as before. Sometimes you have to move on. Jesus felt this pain in John 6:66—one of the saddest verses in the Bible. This is why you take this horrible pain to the Lord, because He really understands and cares.

Forgive and forget. Forgive like Paul teaches us in Ephesians 4:32. Forget like the old apostle wrote in Philippians 4:13–14.

Here's one reason why this happened in your life. Jesus knew that your young disciples would need this teaching one day. You can share your experience of how you handled it with God's help to help them through one of the worst experiences that men and women can have.

Or it is a test, like in the book of Job, and God knew that you and I could handle this just like Job.

Did you think about God wanting to do something in the other person's life and Him using you to help with this? I know it is painful beyond measure (been there, done that). God has the bigger picture in mind. Trust Him on this one.

Another reason needed? This may be hard to fathom, but He may have protected you by getting the other person out of your life. Perhaps you will never know the reason. Check out the chapter called "Let It Go!"

When to Cut Bait

Me? A fisherman? No, I'm not. There is a phrase that fishermen use to describe when it is time to cut bait and put a new hook, sinker, and fresh bait on their line. There are times like this in life and in the ministry.

We don't like to give up on someone or stop a project. Some of us will give it all we've got, stubbornly refusing to cut bait. I admit that cutting bait is a last resort, yet Matthew 18 tells us that if a person refuses and refuses help or church discipline, you finally have to cut bait.

Cut bait? End the relationship. Stop the project. See the chapter called "Let It Go!"

Let's look at a project situation. There are times when you have a vision, a dream, a great idea, but no matter what you do, it just seems to not be working out. You've poured time, energy, and resources into it. You are exhausted and frustrated, questioning yourself and wondering why God has not blessed your project. Not fun.

Proverbs 16:1–3 tells us to make a plan, but don't forget to peruse verse 9 in that chapter. Also, 16:9 is mega important because God evaluates the plan, either moving forward with it or stopping it. Maybe now is just not the right time, so you put the project on the back burner. Maybe this idea is too taxing with not enough resources available, whether it's resources or finances. Perhaps God is just telling you to wait or He used the situation and circumstances to test you. No matter what, don't lose heart.

What about a difficult person? Praying that God will break through the barriers this person has erected or that he or she will stop making life-destroying decisions, you give it to God. Could it be that the other person is not part of the equation anymore? If so, pray and wait a few days, then cut bait.

Yes, I've had to do this because someone would not listen, only wanting to pursue evil. Broke my heart—had to realize that it's time to move on. Now wait, don't use this as the easy way out. Check your heart and your motives, taking this to the Lord in serious prayer. Don't do it in anger. The Lord is looking deep into your heart. God knows our hearts and our thoughts. He even knows what we're going to say before we say it (Psalms 139:4). Think about that!

Why should you cut bait? God's will. Turn the whole matter over to God, trusting Him with a phrase that I use often, "God is at work." I wrote about this in the chapter titled "God Is at Work."

What do you do after you cut bait? Walk away. Move on. For example, I spent many hours trying to keep a staff member from leaving. Lots of conversations. Prayer. I was warned by another staff member that this man had a history of never being satisfied and that I would not be able to get him to be satisfied. I plunged forward in spite of this advice. One afternoon when I was meeting with the disgruntled man, he remarked, "Eric, I feel like we are two ships passing in the night." Upon hearing this, I realized he was not on my ship, and I said goodbye to him.

It was time to cut bait.

You Get What You Inspect, Not What You Expect

Years ago, my mentor was teaching on the topic of job descriptions. After he explained what each leader was to do in the youth meetings, he talked about the importance of the weekly planning meeting. This is a time the volunteer youth leaders meet to plan the next youth meeting, make plans for a monthly activity for the teens, plan evangelism, and so on. One of the items was a quick review of job descriptions during the planning meeting. To amplify the importance of this, he said, "You get what you inspect, not what you expect." That stuck with me.

In the thirteenth chapter of the book of Acts, Paul and Barnabas started on their first missionary journey. Later they returned to Jerusalem to give a report. "And some days after Paul said unto Barnabas, Let us go again and visit our brethren in every city where we have preached the word of the Lord, and see how they do" (Acts 15:36). They could have stayed in Jerusalem, but they wanted to check on their new brothers and sisters in Christ, to see how they were doing. Is this not getting what you inspect rather than what you expect?

My mentor encouraged the youth leaders to bring their Quiet Time Diaries (devotional books) to the planning meeting so the leaders could look at each other's books. This was for the purpose of accountability. If the youth leaders were not willing to have a daily time with the Lord, how could we expect the teens to do so?

We assume that everyone on the team is doing what he or she is supposed to be doing. The reality is that some people don't, for one reason or another. Sad but true. Having to bring Quiet Time Diaries to the leadership team planning meeting was a strong motivation to be faithful. To have someone look at your Quiet Time and see you missed three days since last week? No way!

Same situation with the teenagers regarding their devotional life. You get what you inspect, not what you expect. Teens can see right through adults who are not faithful. It takes them less than a couple of minutes to size up an adult to see if he or she is fake or the real deal. Food for thought.

Staff members—same thing. Check out the chapter called "Catch Someone in the Act of Doing Something Good." Look for the positive as much as possible while thinking about a team member's job description. Catch them performing their job description and praise them for it. This emphasizes that this person is doing what they should be doing and you like this. They will perform at a higher level because of your praise and positive comments. At the same time, you have to evaluate each staff member at least on an annual basis. Better to do this every six months or on a quarterly basis. In doing so, you get what you inspect, not what you expect.

If you think you can recruit a new team member, explain their job description, and assume that it will be done without fail, you are deluded. You should never assume this. Don't assume, inspect. During the first week, check to see how the new person is doing. Does he or she have questions? Anything that they don't understand about their job description? Any problems? Do it again after thirty days with a different set of questions.

"Peter, so glad you are part of our team. From my vantage point, things seem to be going well. How about you on your end?" After your new recruit talks for a bit, bring out the job description. Run through each point, each duty, making some positive comments. If you have a concern, stop there and say, "Hey, Peter, regarding this part of your job description, how is it going? Do you truly understand what you should do here? Let me go over this again." After this review, put him at ease. "Peter, just wanted to make sure you understand what you need to do. Think of it this way. If I don't do my job to check on you to make sure you understand what I'm asking you to do, I would be doing you a great disservice. Please don't be upset because I'm just trying to help you. Once again, welcome to the team!" Big smile and a good handshake. "Wishing you God's best. By the way, I'm praying for you, Peter. Let me know if you have some prayer requests."

Wait for sixty days before doing something like this again, but make certain you drop by their desk or see them in the field to stay in contact. Then sit down with this team member every ninety days. Takes time, yet it is time well spent training your team member. You will be able to sniff out problems before they fester or boil over.

As your team grows, you will be developing supervisors, and you will need to do the same thing for them. Make certain you teach them how to do what you have been doing.

Sit in on a few of these to do an evaluation of your supervisor handling their staff. Then let the supervisor do these meetings alone. Start meeting with your supervisors to talk about the overall business or ministry plan, progress, goals, and so on. One of the topics will be staff—time to inspect. Ask the supervisors how their staff members are doing. Plans can be made to retrain some staff, evaluate their performance, and more.

What you are doing is expanding your ministry or your business. You cannot do everything. So grow and develop your team. At some point, you will be managing managers, then division heads (2 Tim. 2:2).

Young Leaders

In 1 Timothy 4:12, it says, "Let no man despise thy youth; but be thou an example of the believers, in word, in conversation, in charity, in spirit, in faith, in purity."

Those who were once younger, remembering their own mistakes, either have low expectations of you, dismissing you because they are not patient with you, or they have expectations that are too high. Sometimes so high it is nearly impossible to please them. What do you do?

To paraphrase 1 Timothy 4:12, don't give anyone an opportunity to look down on you because you are young. Instead, be an example of the believers, in ministry, in your lifestyle, loving others, in spirit, in faith, and in purity.

Be an excellent example in everything that you do. Look at it this way: everything you do, do it as if Jesus Christ is your boss. In a way, He is. I'm sure that if Jesus were standing next to us, both you and I would work harder and push ourselves to be excellent in everything that we do.

Truth be known, some older leaders are going to look down on you no matter what you do. Just grin and bear it, doing so with a sweet attitude. In due time, they will notice your hard work and your passion for excellence. In doing so, you will grow and mature. Paul had this attitude regarding John Mark in the beginning, but he changed his opinion when he saw the growth in the younger man.

Is there a shortcut? Maybe. Develop the habit of reading a chapter from Proverbs every day. Look at the warnings, choosing what is right. Literally run away from what is bad. Day after day in Proverbs will allow God's wisdom to permeate your heart and soul. Wise actions will begin to flow out of you. It *will* be noticed.

What not to do? Don't chafe about this process. Just accept it from God as a learning experience. If you develop a bad attitude, it will become evident, and you will be looked down upon. This will only frustrate you. What are some negative characteristics of being young? Haste, waste, being sensitive or easily offended, acting silly all the time, rejecting rebuke or reproof, arrogance, pride, being a know-it-all, rejecting authority, being rebellious—bad list. What to do? Basically, just the opposite of this list. Choose the positive characteristics such as high energy, hard work, drive, determination, patience, good attitude, listening and heeding rebuke, being respectful, being agreeable, having humility, knowing how far to go (joking, teasing) and when to stop, being obedient—good list.

Want to gain the attention of someone older? Ask good, smart questions to show you are a learner. Take notes and implement the best ideas so the older person will see that you are serious.

When does a man become a man? I know a man in his late sixties who is immature and selfish. Age-wise, he is a man. Not sure if he qualifies in the biblical sense. Age thirty? Thirty-five? Forty? Oops, I forgot twenty-one. Hebrews considered a man to be a man when he was forty, yet Jesus began His public ministry at age thirty. Joseph became the prime minister of Egypt at age thirty. There is no magical number. A man shows evidence of becoming a man when he pursues God with all of his heart. Daily reading and memory work in Proverbs will help you.

Keep doing this and suddenly, one day, others will begin to say, "You know, you are a man now. You're no longer a boy." I kindly suggest that you should not tell others that you are a man now. If so, you just proved otherwise.

You Will Not Believe What We Prayed For

Talk about an unglamorous prayer meeting.

We wanted to expand our meeting room by adding a stage or platform for our speakers, musicians, and drama team. It was just a few months after the Berlin Wall came down and Hungary became a free nation. We had volunteer work teams from Germany, Poland, and Transylvania (the Hungarian-speaking section of Romania) as well as some Hungarians helping us. We had five languages being spoken in and around our meeting room—German, Polish, Hungarian, Romanian—with me speaking English. Sounds like the Tower of Babel, doesn't it?

The Polish team was working on the new entry while the Germans worked on the stage area. Hungarians and Romanians were working in other areas of the building or around the property. We came to a standstill because of a major problem. We needed to remove a support beam and add a steel I-bar to hold up a span about twenty feet long. But such a piece of steel was not available anywhere in the country at that time.

In modern Hungary, there are many building supply stores providing many choices. Not so in early 1990 in Hungary. We looked and looked. Not available. We were desperate. It was time to pray. Can you imagine us on our knees, praying for a long piece of steel? God is interested in all of our needs.

During the prayer meeting, God gave me an idea. I stopped praying, tapping the arm of our staff member who was overseeing all construction and maintenance. He told me that he was not finished praying. I tapped him again, telling him that God just gave me a great idea. He opened his eyes, giving me a suspicious look. "My brother, I speak in a different church every Sunday. After the service, one of the families invites me to eat with them. I've noticed that all of them have stacks of building materials in their

185

backyards. Tiles, bricks, wood, pieces of steel—stop right there. Steel? My dear friend, somebody somewhere in Hungary has a piece of steel about twenty feet long, sitting in their backyard, and you need to go find it."

"That's a wonderful idea, Eric. God has indeed spoken to you. I have some contacts. I will ask around. I must go at once. Keep praying."

Would you believe that he returned in less than two hours with exactly what we needed? I kid you not. In those days, sometimes he would use the barter system to pay for things. Trade something that we had to get something that we needed. He told me that we had a lot of potatoes and onions, which was exactly what this family needed. They were so happy to receive the food. Can you imagine our joy when he brought the steel to the meeting room? The Poles and Germans were whooping it up, yelling praise to God. The Hungarians and Romanians shook their heads in disbelief. They *knew* how difficult it was to find certain things in the country. I was ecstatic, and our dear brother Bela Patkai was rejoicing. Bela was so kind to take a sabbatical from the pastorate for four years to help us in our early days. After returning to the pastorate for a number of years, he went to be with our Lord. I always enjoyed praying with him—especially the day when we prayed for a long piece of steel.

Then there was the time that we had a prayer meeting to find twenty-four toilet bowls. Would you believe that there was not even one new toilet bowl in Hungary at that time? Another prayer meeting—another idea—another answer to prayer.

Conclusion

I keep thinking, *Oh, I need to tell them about this story and that one.* Truth is I have a list with more than seventy-five more stories. Another book? God only knows.

In closing, Moses stood at the Red Sea listening to the whining and crying of the Israelites who feared imminent death or capture by the Egyptians. Pharaoh and his army were bearing down upon them. The rugged mountains prevented them from going south or turning west. To the north were the Egyptians. To the east, the Red Sea. Moses prayed, but God stopped him, asking why he was praying and saying that he should take the next step—into the Red Sea. What a step of faith it was! When Moses obeyed, God parted the waters, and the rest is history.

So, my friend, I have one last thing to say to you now that you have read this book. "Take the next step!" Use what God put on my heart to get you going, moving forward—to take the next step.

References

"Death of a Spouse"
1) Marc Batterson, *Draw the Circle* (Zondervan, 2012), 34.
2) Ibid.

"Let It Go!"
3) Transcribed from *The Battle Is the Lord's*, Pastor T. D. Jakes, sermon preached in 2005 in Houston, Texas.

"Listen Up!"
4) Quote from *Taking Men Alive*, booklet by C. G Trumbull.
5) Ibid.

"Set the Pace"
6) Lee Roberson quote from a sermon by Dr. Lee Roberson, deceased pastor, Highland Park Baptist Church, Chattanooga, Tennessee, <u>fundamentalbaptistsermons.net.</u>

How to Have a Personal Relationship with God

God truly loves you and wants to have a personal relationship with you. In fact, He took the first step toward you by giving His Son, Jesus Christ, to die on the cross for your sins. If you do not have a relationship with God I kindly ask you to consider praying this prayer.

"Dear God, I realize that I am a sinner and I am very sorry for my sins. Please forgive me of my sins. I believe that Jesus Christ is Your Son and that You raised Him from the grave. I put my faith and trust in You asking You to come into my heart and life to save me from my sins. Thank You."

If you prayed this prayer I would love to hear from you so I can encourage you and pray for you.

Printed in the United States
By Bookmasters